Praying with the Anabaptists

*The Secret of
Bearing Fruit*

Marlene Kropf & Eddy Hall

P R E S S

Newton, Kansas
Winnipeg, Manitoba

Praying with the Anabaptists: The Secret of Bearing Fruit

Unless otherwise noted, all Scripture quotations are from the New Revised Standard Version Bible, copyright © 1989, by the Division of Christian Education of the National Council of the Churches of Christ in the USA, and used by permission.

Printed in the United States of America

97 96 95 94 4 3 2 1

Library of Congress Number 94-71733
International Standard Book Number 0-87303-246-2

Editorial direction for Faith & Life Press by Susan E. Janzen; copyediting by Melanie Mueller and Jennifer Stultz; book design by Gwen M. Stamm; printing by Mennonite Press.

Contents

Foreword

HERE, AT LAST, is a guide to prayer that comes out of the fires of Anabaptist spirituality. It has always been apparent that the early martyrs must have had the power of prayer behind their witness, but never before has the written witness of their personal relationships with God been brought together for the purpose of guiding us in developing our own prayer lives.

In these pages, Anabaptism is not merely recounted history—it comes alive! This guide revisits the writings of the sixteenth-century martyrs and leaders of the Anabaptist movement to discover time-honored yet refreshing ways to deepen our practice of prayer. True to the spirit of Anabaptism, it focuses not merely on accomplishing the task of prayer but on the relationship to be found with God through prayer. And it does this in terms that can speak not only to today's heirs of the Anabaptist movement—Mennonites, Brethren, Amish, and Hutterites—but to all who seek a more intimate relationship with God.

This is not a book to be read in a race with time. It is an invitation to meet the Spirit of Jesus Christ. In this book you will find many ways of encountering God: Scripture, biblical meditations, quotes from Anabaptists, stories, written prayers, prayer exercises, and hymns. A companion cassette recording of the selected hymns, as performed by the Chamber Singers of Eastern Mennonite University, enhances the value of this guide for those whose spirits are fed by sacred music. Each person's favorite way of meeting God will be found here as well as new ways of praying which can enrich beyond previous experience.

I invite you to make a date with God and take this book along as a guide for your words, imaginations, silence, and listening. When your soul meets God's, stop. Don't feel compelled to push ahead to finish the chapter, the page, or even the sentence; relish the moment.

Or you may prefer to follow this guide with others. Listening to the meditations and doing the prayer exercises in a group can heighten their power. When a leader guides the group, participants' imaginations are freed to enter fully into prayer and meditation without interruptions. In addition, belonging to a group that prays together can greatly enrich each person's individual prayer life and strengthen each one to live in Christ-like ways during all the ordinary moments of the week.

Before you turn to the first meditations, ask God to increase your desire to pray. As you read and listen, expect to be met by the living Christ. Then as you let go of written and spoken words, let the Holy Spirit transform the rest of your day into unceasing prayer as you live in awareness of being in communion with God.

Sandra Drescher-Lehman
Richmond, Virginia

Praying with the Anabaptists

A SURPRISING TREND in recent years has been the wide-spread revival of interest in prayer. Half a century ago many churches held midweek prayer meetings. Today few do. Yet in every corner of the land people are asking how to pray.

Spiritual retreat centers have sprung up in many places. Schools are offering courses in prayer. Spiritual direction, an ancient ministry of the church, is being practiced again as people seek guidance for deepening their life of prayer.

What many people are recognizing is that the listening modes of prayer have been neglected. We are good at making requests of God but not so good at hearing God speak to us. Twentieth-century Christians have become so infected by the busy, productive spirit of our age that we have almost abandoned prayer in our pursuit of accomplishment.

Prayer as Abiding in the Vine

Not accomplishment but relationship is at the heart of prayer—an intimate, trusting relationship between the Creator and the children of earth. Jesus used a vivid image to speak of our relationship with God:

Abide in me as I abide in you.
I am the vine, you are the branches.
John 15:4-5

Jesus went on to expand the image—to describe God as a wise, patient Gardener and himself as the sturdy, life-giving vine. Such an image echoes many Old Testament texts. In Israel's oldest story, God planted a garden—a fruitful place of trees, a river, and pleasant breezes. Israel's poets and prophets also described God as a gardener—one who carefully tends the land and nourishes great hopes for Israel, God's beloved vine. The prophet Isaiah wrote:

A pleasant vineyard, sing about it!
I, the Lord, am its keeper;
   every moment I water it.
I guard it night and day
   so that no one can harm it.

In days to come Jacob shall take root,
   Israel shall blossom and put forth shoots,
   and fill the whole world with fruit.
Isaiah 27:2-3,6

But over and over again, Israel disappointed the Vinegrower. Instead of bringing forth a harvest of justice and righteousness, Israel turned away from God and failed to keep the covenant. The prophet Jeremiah spoke of God's disappointment in a lament:

Yet I planted you as a choice vine,
  from the purest stock.
How then did you turn degenerate
  and become a wild vine?
Jeremiah 2:21

Although the vineyard of Israel often failed to fulfill God's hopes, Jesus proclaims himself as the "true vine," the one who inaugurates God's new day and ushers in a reign of righteousness and peace. As the true vine, Jesus lived in complete harmony with God's purposes and God's dream of wholeness and fruitfulness. His life of loving ministry bore the clear imprint of God's own gracious character. The invitation heard by the disciples in John 15 is an astonishing call to become one with God—just as Jesus had been one with God.

The same invitation is offered to us. We too are called to abide in the vine, to make our home in Christ, to dwell in a rich, satisfying relationship that produces abundant fruit. At the heart of such a relationship is a vital life of prayer.

An Anabaptist Rule for Prayer and the Spiritual Life

Several centuries ago an Anabaptist leader, Pilgram Marpeck, wrote a meditation in which he described springtime in God's vineyard:

The vines have sprouted blossoms and exude fragrance, that is, the planting of the heavenly Father which He has planted as the true Gardener in Jesus Christ, the true vine. The shoots from the vine which are planted are the true believers in Christ Jesus. Through the sap of grace from Christ the vine, they develop blossoms that they may see God's working in them through His plantings in Christ and give God praise, in Christ Jesus (HAAS, p. 129).

Marpeck was a member of the Anabaptists, a new religious movement in Europe in the early 1500s. These fervent Christians tried to follow Jesus daily and live in harmony and intimacy with one another. Many of them were persecuted for their faith, and over 4,000 eventually died as martyrs. In the letters they wrote from prison they gave eloquent testimony to their deeply rooted faith and encouraged their sisters and brothers to remain true to Christ. Some of their prayers are included in this book.

Out of the Anabaptists' devotion and suffering, a "rule" or comprehensive vision for faithful Christian living emerged. In keeping with Jesus' counsel to his disciples in John 13-17, the rule consists of three fundamental movements:

- A vital, personal relationship with Jesus Christ sustained by prayer and other spiritual disciplines;

- A wholehearted, loving commitment to life in

Christian community sustained through corporate worship, mutual care and discernment, and sharing of life;

· Joyfully following Christ's way in the world through a holy life of witness, service and peacemaking—even through suffering.

The three-pronged Anabaptist "rule of life" was permeated with prayer. Though the leaders did not leave specific instructions or guidance for teaching people to pray, believers were expected to live in daily communion with God. In writing of the requirements for baptism, Balthasar Hubmaier noted that the candidates "must be able to pray" (KLAASSEN, p. 121).

Walter of Stoelwijk, who was martyred in 1541, wrote from prison: "Now if Christ Jesus our Lord frequently spent whole nights in prayer, and also prayed in the garden before His death, we should also pray without ceasing, especially in our distress" (VAN BRAGHT, p. 464).

From her prison cell in Flanders in 1560, Soetgen Van Den Houte wrote to her children before her death as a martyr, "Be diligent in prayer and love the poor...engage yourselves with psalms, hymns, and spiritual songs...." She pointed them to the example of Daniel and his three friends who "walked in the ways of the Lord, with prayer and supplication..." (VAN BRAGHT, p. 647).

Singing as a Mode of Prayer

For the Anabaptists, an important way of experiencing and expressing God's presence was through singing hymns. Even while in prison or on their way to the stake of martyrdom, they confidently sang their faith. In 1546, for example, four Anabaptists (Hans Staudtach, Antony Keyn, Blasius Beck, and Leonhard Schneider) were condemned to death and delivered to the executioner.

> When they were being led out to the slaughter, they boldly and joyfully sang.... The brethren then knelt down and fervently prayed, offering up this burnt offering as their final farewell to the world.... They then blessed each other and exhorted one another to steadfastness, to be strong and of good cheer, saying, "Today we shall be together in the kingdom of our heavenly Father." (VAN BRAGHT, p. 475)

In 1550 another group of four—two men and two women—were led to their execution in Brabant in the province of Antwerp, Belgium. Standing in a circle they knelt down, prayed, and kissed each other. One of them, Anneken, immediately began to sing, "In thee, O Lord, do I put my trust" (Psalm 71:1). When the executioner's assistants told her to be still, another member of the group named Govert said, "No, sister, sing on," and helped her sing. The bailiff was enraged at this response and ordered Govert to be gagged. However, Govert held his teeth so firmly closed that the gag did not hinder him much and he laughingly said, "I could easily sing with the gag on; but Paul says: 'Sing in your heart to God'" (Ephesians 5:19) (VAN BRAGHT, p. 495).

A particularly poignant story comes from the city of Nijmegen, Holland, in the summer of 1556 where Gerrit Hasepoot, a tailor, was sentenced to death. When his wife came to see him for the last time, she could hardly hold their infant in her arms because of her great grief.

When he was led to death, and having been brought from the wagon upon the scaffold, he lifted up his voice and sang the hymn:

Father in heaven, I call:
  Oh, strengthen now my faith.

Thereupon he fell upon his knees and fervently prayed to God. Having been placed at the stake, he kicked his slippers from his feet, saying: "It were a pity to burn them for they can be of service still to some poor person." The rope with which he was to be strangled, becoming a little loose, having not been twisted well by the executioner, he again lifted up his voice and sang the end of said hymn:

Brethren, sisters, all, good-bye!
  We now must separate,
Till we meet beyond the sky,

With Christ our only Head:
For this yourselves prepare,
And I'll await you there (VAN BRAGHT, p. 560).

The many descendants of the Anabaptists treasured these stories and hymns and found singing to be one of the richest, most fruitful modes of personal and communal prayer. Although the Anabaptist tradition did not produce many written prayer books, their hymnals in effect became their prayer books.

In this guide to prayer, a hymn has been selected to accompany each meditation. Many people have discovered that singing or listening to hymns is a helpful way to center their attention on God. As we sing, our hearts become quiet, and we are able to hear God speak and also express our own devotion to God. Hymns can either be sung or listened to on the accompanying cassette tape.

How to Use This Guide to Prayer

Because prayer is an intimate relationship, it takes time. This book has been developed to provide direction for expanding and deepening a life of prayer with God. It can be used on a daily or weekly basis. It can be used by an individual or a small group. It could serve as a guide for a study group.

Each meditation includes a selected scripture from John 13–17 with reflections on the text, a hymn, words from the early Anabaptists, and a martyr's prayer. Each meditation is followed by a guided prayer exercise to lead you deeper into God's presence. Some will find the keeping of a journal to be another helpful tool in their practice of prayer.

The prayers of the martyrs and some of the Anabaptist quotations have been adapted and revised for easier reading. The suggestions for ways to pray have been gathered from the wider Christian prayer tradition.

• In *Part One: Abiding in the Vine*, the prayer exercises focus on one's personal relationship with God through Christ. These are quiet, reflective modes of prayer that emphasize listening.

• In *Part Two: Joined in Love*, the prayer exercises expand to include the larger Christian community. Not only one's relationship with God, but one's relationships with sisters and brothers in the church become the focus. Prayer becomes a way of loving others.

• In *Part Three: Bearing Fruit*, one's life of ministry is the focus of prayer. Prayer becomes a way of joining with God's loving, creative, liberating work in the world.

Any prayer guide for Mennonites would have to include music. Singing and prayer are so intimately linked that it would be unthinkable to offer guidelines for prayer that did not give attention to music. The hymns accompanying each of the chapters were chosen from *Hymnal: A Worship Book*, the Mennonites' most recent hymnal.

Not every attempt to pray will be fruitful. Menno Simons, an early Anabaptist, wrote, "I confess that often my prayer is mixed with sin" (WENGER, p. 67). Sometimes you will struggle to be open to God's voice. Sometimes you may resist the guidance you receive. At other times you may neglect prayer because of work or family demands.

The important thing is to come back and start again. God wants to be in relationship with you—wants to be your truest, dearest friend. If you cultivate the discipline of regular prayer, you will be rewarded with the joy of nearness to God and a life of fruitfulness.

May all of us grow closer to Christ as we continue to learn to pray!

Sources Cited in this Book

THE QUOTES from Anabaptists and the martyrs' prayers in this book are adapted from the sources listed on this page. The names in parenthesis following the sources are the abbreviations that appear within the text of the book.

Because most of the material used from these sources originated several hundred years ago, some of the vocabulary and style features may seem archaic to modern readers. To aid in understanding, the writers and editors of this book decided to change some words and phrases into current terminology. Every attempt has been made to remain faithful to the intent and meaning of the original authors.

Anabaptism in Outline: Selected Primary Sources. Edited by Walter Klaassen. Classics of the Radical Reformation, no.3. Scottdale, PA: Herald Press, 1981. (KLAASSEN)

The Complete Writings of Menno Simons. Translated by Leonard Verduin. Edited by J.C. Wenger. Scottdale, PA: Herald Press, 1956. (WENGER)

The Bloody Theater or Martyrs Mirror of the Defenseless Christians, Twelfth Edition. Thieleman J. van Braght. Translated by Joseph F. Sohm in 1886. Scottdale, PA: Herald Press, 1979. (VAN BRAGHT)

Hymnal: A Worship Book. Elgin, IL: Brethren Press, Newton, KS: Faith & Life Press, Scottdale, PA: Mennonite Publishing House, 1992. (HWB)

Lifesigns. Henri J. Nouwen. New York: Doubleday & Company, 1986. (NOUWEN)

Readings from Mennonite Writings, New and Old. J. Craig Haas. Intercourse, PA: Good Books, 1992. (HAAS)

Selected Writings of Hans Denck 1500-1527. Translated and edited by Edward J. Furcha. Texts and studies in religion, vol. 44. Lewiston, NY: The Edwin Mellen Press, Ltd., 1989. (FURCHA)

Spiritual Legacy of Hans Denck: Interpretation & Translation of Key Texts. Clarence Bauman. Studies in Medieval & Reformation Thought, vol. 47. Kinderhook, NY: E.J. Brill, 1990. (BAUMAN)

Smith's Story of the Mennonites. C. Henry Smith. Fifth Edition. Revised and Enlarged by Cornelius Krahn. Newton, KS: Faith & Life Press, 1981. (SMITH)

The Writings of Pilgram Marpeck. Translated and edited by William Klassen and Walter Klaassen. Classics of the Radical Reformation, no. 2. Scottdale, PA: Herald Press, 1978. (MARPECK)

Introducing the Creators of the Prayer Guide

A WORD ABOUT the people who gave birth to this guide. In 1990 the General Conference Mennonite Church and the Mennonite Church responded to a desire for spiritual renewal by appointing a Spirituality Reference Council. The council was co-chaired by Norma Johnson of the Commission of Education, Newton, Kansas, and Marlene Kropf of the Mennonite Board of Congregational Ministries, Elkhart, Indiana. Four additional members were John R. Martin of Eastern Mennonite Seminary, Harrisonburg, Virginia; Marcus Smucker of Associated Mennonite Biblical Seminary, Elkhart, Indiana; John Lenshyn, pastor of Foothills Mennonite Church, Calgary, Alberta; and Laurence Martin of Mennonite Publishing House, Scottdale, Pennsylvania.

The council noted a growing interest in prayer among Mennonites and heard requests for Anabaptist teaching and spiritual guidance. Although many Mennonites regularly find their way to Catholic retreat centers or to evangelical prayer groups, others are reluctant to leave the security of their own church to seek such guidance elsewhere.

Because the council was convinced that much wisdom

about prayer and spiritual growth could be found among the sixteenth-century Anabaptists, they committed themselves to do a personal search of these early writings. Along with this assignment, they chose to focus on John 13—17 as a biblical foundation. When they brought together the Anabaptist prayers and quotations they had collected and set them alongside these biblical themes, they discovered a delightful convergence: the heart of Jesus' message to his disciples about the spiritual life was the same vision upheld by the Anabaptists. The council described this vision as a "rule of life" (see earlier description) and developed it as an organizing principle for a book.

In March 1992 council members met for a write-in at Dogwood Cabin, a lakeside retreat in southern Michigan generously shared by Leroy and Phyllis Troyer of South Bend, Indiana. First drafts of the chapters of this book were written at the cabin and later passed on to Eddy Hall, a freelance writer from Goessel, Kansas, and Marlene Kropf for rewriting and editing. Artist Gwen Stamm of Mennonite Publishing House also participated in the discussions at Dogwood Cabin. Later Susan E. Janzen, editorial director for Faith & Life Press, Newton, Kansas, contributed her skills to the book. Jennifer Stultz, editorial assistant for Faith & Life Press, compiled the biographies of early Anabaptists.

Ken Nafziger, music editor for *Hymnal: A Worship Book*, gave generous support to the project by directing the Chamber Singers of Eastern Mennonite University, Harrisonburg, Virginia, and producing the audio-cassette tape that accompanies this book.

The Spirituality Reference Council must be credited for the central vision and inspiration of this book. In addition, several members of the council served as readers of the manuscript and offered valuable counsel. Without their insight and commitment, the project would never have come to be.

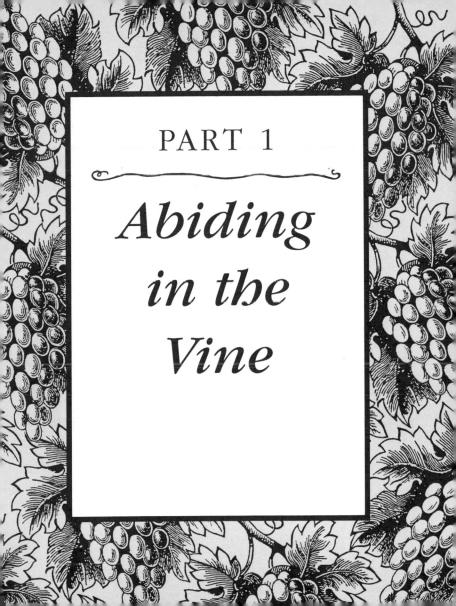

PART 1

Abiding in the Vine

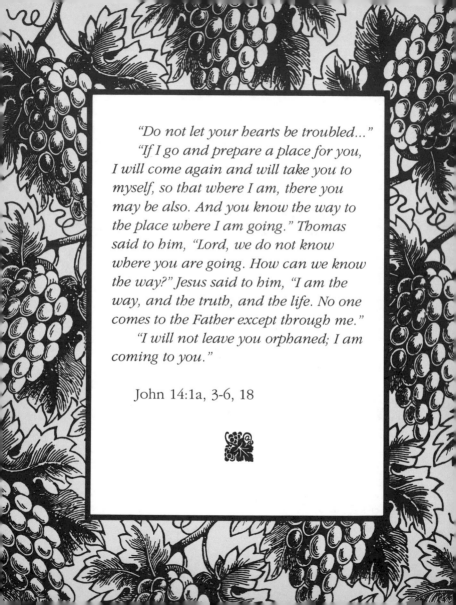

"Do not let your hearts be troubled..."
"If I go and prepare a place for you,
I will come again and will take you to
myself, so that where I am, there you
may be also. And you know the way to
the place where I am going." Thomas
said to him, "Lord, we do not know
where you are going. How can we know
the way?" Jesus said to him, "I am the
way, and the truth, and the life. No one
comes to the Father except through me."
"I will not leave you orphaned; I am
coming to you."

John 14:1a, 3-6, 18

1

Searching for Faith in Troubled Times

So long as life is mostly pleasant, safe, and predictable, most of us can go quite a while without puzzling over ultimate questions of meaning and purpose. We can easily accept the answers put forth by this catechism or that, family tradition, or even car manufacturers.

But when grief or suffering invade, when security is stripped away, when the familiar crumbles beneath the advance of ever-accelerating change, the easy answers of others no longer satisfy. Our spirits cry out, "Why is this happening to me? What can I hold onto? Where do I go from here?"

Ours is a day that thrusts such questions upon us. Science, technology, and education, which once promised uninterrupted social progress, have proven impotent as saviors. Where then do we look for hope for our future?

The breakdown of national moral consensus leaves us wondering how, or even whether, we can effectively govern ourselves. Is truth something that changes with every opinion poll?

The "good life"—marked by widespread affluence and unprecedented leisure—leaves us disappointed with its shallowness. Is this as good as it gets? Is there nothing more?

Though the turmoil of our time bombards us with such questions, the questions are hardly new. Some years ago a man named Thomas sought earnestly to devote his life only to what truly counted. Never one to accept easy answers, he asked for clarification when he didn't understand. When presented with unsubstantiated claims, he demanded proof. Thomas's slowness to believe, though, came not from any fear of commitment, but from a determination to live only for what was true, only for what really mattered.

Then into Thomas's life came Jesus of Nazareth, who completely won the cautious Israelite's loyalty. In a world full of the false promises Thomas was so adept at seeing through, Jesus was authentic.

Jesus' vision of God's rule inspired Thomas's total allegiance. In Jesus, Thomas believed, all Israel's hopes would be fulfilled, and along with them, his own. Thomas found Jesus himself entirely credible—a man of complete integrity whose greater-than-human love presented an exhilarating contrast to the petty selfishness he saw all around him, even among most religious leaders. Little wonder, then, that Thomas left everything to follow him.

Thomas followed Jesus for two and a half years, watching him, learning from him, assisting him. At first a disciple, in time Thomas became a friend, an intimate friend. And then Jesus, who by then had become Thomas's very reason for living, announced the unthinkable: "I'm going away."

Thomas had been ready to die with Jesus, so great was his loyalty (John 11:16), but for Jesus to leave him behind, to abandon him, was something else altogether. What of this "kingdom of God" that had only begun to appear in tiniest measure? Was Jesus aborting his mission after having just begun it? But more importantly to Thomas at that moment, what of their friendship? What kind of friend shares ever more deeply of himself, inviting the other to greater and greater intimacy and commitment, then abruptly leaves?

Thomas's world was quaking beneath his feet. It was a moment for ultimate questions.

Jesus told Thomas, along with the other ten disciples, that they knew the way to where he was going. Thomas found these words hollow comfort and didn't hesitate to say so: "Lord, we do not know where you are going. How can we know the way?"

Thomas's candor elicited one of Jesus' greatest pronouncements ever: "I am the way, the truth, and the life. No one comes to the Father except through me." With these words Jesus revealed not only that he was going to the Father and that he, in some sense, was the way they too could connect with God; he also answered Thomas's ultimate questions—and those of our age as well.

To all who search for direction, Jesus says, "I am the way."
To all who yearn for meaning, Jesus says, "I am the truth."
To all who seek purpose for living, Jesus says, "I am the life."

But if Jesus could have offered Thomas only answers, that would have been small consolation. Jesus was leaving! Answers, even profound answers, could not fill that void. It could be filled by only one thing: Jesus' presence.

And that's exactly what Jesus promised. "I will not leave you orphaned," he said, "I am coming to you." Thomas would not understand until Pentecost just how Jesus would fulfill this promise, but it spoke to Thomas's most compelling need. And to ours.

Yes, in troubled times we desperately need direction. We need meaning. We need purpose. But most of all, we need to know that we are constantly companioned by the One who gives direction and meaning and purpose—the One who is the Way, the Truth, and the Life.

And so, to all of us who share Thomas' longings, Jesus offers the greatest gift of all—himself.

Anabaptist Voices

Like Jesus' first disciples, the Anabaptists of the early sixteenth century discovered a faith that met the challenges of troubled times. Though they were often persecuted and driven from their homes, they experienced the daily, comforting presence of the risen Christ among them. Perhaps nowhere is the secret of their faith expressed so clearly as in the often-quoted statement by

Hans Denck, an Anabaptist leader in South Germany,

> "No one can truly know [Christ] unless [one] follows
> him in life, and no one may follow him unless [one]
> has first known him" (KLAASSEN, p. 87).

To know Christ and to follow Christ were inseparable
realities for the Anabaptists. As they came to know Christ
intimately as friend and guide, they responded by living as
Christ's friends in the world. They became a loving, holy
people who remained committed to Christ even in the
face of great danger.

Guided Prayer Exercise: Prayer of Reflection

The disciples enjoyed daily interaction with Jesus. They
walked many miles together, shared meals, heard Jesus
teach and tell stories, saw him heal the sick, and joined
him in prayer. Today the Spirit of Jesus continues to live
among his followers, and we too can know Jesus in the
ordinary events of our lives.

One of the ways Christians through the centuries have
come to recognize the presence of Jesus is by a simple
prayer of reflection at the end of the day. In this prayer the
day's events are reviewed with "eyes of faith" to discover
how and where God has been at work.

If you want to pray the prayer of reflection, follow
these steps:

1. Listen to the hymn "We walk by faith" (Hymnal, 570).

2. Pray for openness to the light of God's Spirit as you reflect on the day just past.

3. Look back over your day and quietly recall each event or encounter. How did you experience God's love and grace? Give thanks for all you received from God's hand.

4. Become aware of your hunger or desire for God in this day. How did you reach out to God? If you struggled to live in peace and hope, confess your desire for a deeper sense of Christ's presence. If you become aware of sin, seek forgiveness and cleansing.

5. What do you sense God is calling you to be and do tomorrow? Ask for grace to follow Christ in all things. Give yourself into God's care. Rest in the comfort of God's everlasting love.

6. Close your time of prayer by singing or listening to the hymn "We walk by faith."

Martyr's Prayer

In early February 1538, a faithful Christian named Walter of Stoelwijk was imprisoned and brought to trial in Brabant, Belgium. For three years he endured great suffering and torture, yet remained steadfast in the faith. In a letter written from prison, he quoted the apostle Paul who wrote, "Blessed be the God and Father of our Lord Jesus Christ, the Father of mercies and the God of all consolation, who consoles us in all our affliction" (2 Corinthians 1:3-4a). Finally on March 24, 1541, he was sentenced and burned at the stake.

Prayer of Walter of Stoelwijk

Merciful Father, look upon me with eyes of compassion,...
  for to You only ... belongs praise and honor....
I commit soul and body into your divine and gracious
keeping:
  guide me, through Jesus Christ your dear Son,
    into all things that are well pleasing
      to your divine Spirit....
Preserve us by your divine Word now and forever. Amen.
                              (VAN BRAGHT, p. 464)

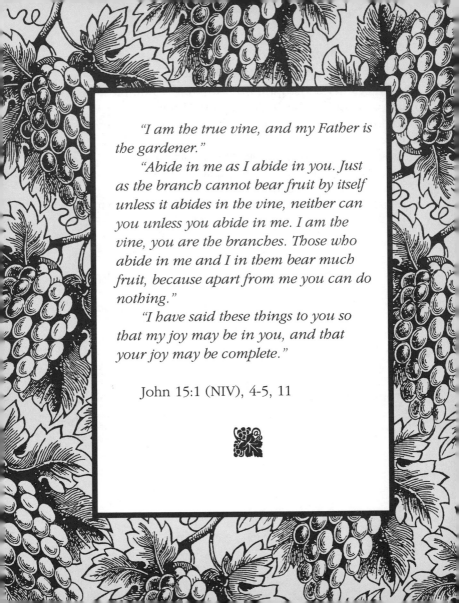

"I am the true vine, and my Father is the gardener."

"Abide in me as I abide in you. Just as the branch cannot bear fruit by itself unless it abides in the vine, neither can you unless you abide in me. I am the vine, you are the branches. Those who abide in me and I in them bear much fruit, because apart from me you can do nothing."

"I have said these things to you so that my joy may be in you, and that your joy may be complete."

John 15:1 (NIV), 4-5, 11

2

Making Our Home in Christ

W HEN THE NEW STAFF member didn't hang pictures in his office, his coworkers just assumed he wasn't the interior-decorating type. In reality, by not fully settling into his new office, he was refusing to act at home in a job where he didn't feel at home. Each day his bare walls reminded him, "You're just passing through," and so somehow made it a bit easier to endure in a job that didn't feel like a good fit.

When the worker moved on to a new job, a job he was excited about, pictures immediately appeared on his office walls. Here he wasn't just passing through. He was at home.

There is probably no more universal human longing than the desire to feel at home, to be in a place where we feel safe, accepted, secure, comfortable. Yet ours is a generation that feels less and less at home.

Our post-industrial economy requires a highly mobile workforce. While our great-grandparents may have moved only once or twice in their lifetimes, we expect to move, on the average, about once every five years. About the time we start to sink roots in a community, many of us uproot and move on. After a couple of such uprootings, some of us decide it's less painful to avoid putting down roots.

Even if we move less often, we may struggle to feel at home. As our technological society changes faster and faster, our capacity to adapt is forever being stretched. Even if we don't go anywhere, as the world changes around us we may find ourselves becoming strangers in our own worlds.

A sense of "inner homelessness" may prompt us to move in and out of relationships, change jobs, go back to school, switch churches, or move across the country. Sometimes such moves help, but often they leave us disappointed, feeling no more at home than before.

To those of us who long for a place to belong, Jesus announces good news. He wants to be our home. The Jerusalem Bible translates John 15:4, "Make your home in me, as I make mine in you."

Nowhere does Jesus invite us to intimacy with him more vividly than in the parable of the vine and the branches. Jesus is the vine, we are the branches. We, the branches, can only find our true place by abiding in the vine. What does Jesus mean by this image of abiding?

When a branch is grafted onto a vine, the branch sends out little roots and fibers that grow into the stem. The stem also grows up into the branch until the wood of the vine and the wood of the branch become one. At the same time the sap of the vine enters the branch and flows through it to produce new shoots and leaves and fruit. This organic union is the picture of the relationship to which Jesus invites us.

Jesus invites us to share in his purposes. The branch does not come to the vine with its own agenda; it exists only to fulfill the purpose of the vine–bearing fruit. How often have we decided, without consulting God, what we wanted to do, then asked God to help us achieve it? That is not abiding. To abide, we must yield ourselves to God's purposes.

Jesus invites us to depend on him. "Just as the branch cannot bear fruit by itself unless it abides in the vine," Jesus says, "neither can you unless you abide in me." The branch is completely dependent on the vine.

There is within most of us something that balks at Jesus' pronouncement, "Apart from me you can do nothing." Even if we don't say so, we feel that by our own wit and willpower and work we can accomplish important things. The result of such human effort may look good, may even look like fruit, but in reality it has no lasting value. Only through surrendering to God's purposes and depending on God to fulfill those purposes through us can we become bearers of good fruit.

Jesus invites us to joy. Jesus calls us to exchange our purposes for his and to give up our independence for dependence on him, not so he can be a killjoy, but "so that my joy may be in you, and that your joy may be complete." As Jesus' life flows through us, even as the life of the vine flows through the branch, we become not only fruitbearers, but joyful fruitbearers. As we fulfill the purpose for which God created us, we experience a deep contentment. Through losing our lives, we find life.

As we say yes to Jesus' invitation to shared purposes and dependence on him, we experience the only truly satisfying answer to the restlessness of inner homelessness—the joy that comes from making our home in Christ.

Anabaptist Voices

Soon after his call to ministry sometime during the winter of 1536-37, Menno Simons wrote his "Meditation on the Twenty-Fifth Psalm," part of which is printed here. Similar in form and spirit to the "Confessions" of Augustine (early fifth century), Menno's meditation is an outpouring of a grateful heart. He confesses his sin and youthful wandering away from God and pleads for God's safekeeping in the future. As he praises the God of mercy and grace who delivered him, he expresses his deep conviction that those who know God will dwell forever in God's house of peace.

Meditation on Psalm 25:13

O Lord of hosts,
   this is the final reward for those who know you.
Their souls shall inherit that which is good
   in the paradise of their God.
They are delivered from ... sin [and] death...

and they serve before you in peace and joy of heart
  all their days.
They sleep without fear,
  for you are their strength and shield.
They rest under the shadow of your wings,
  for they are yours.
They fear not,
  for you warm them with the rays of your love.
They hunger not,
  for you feed them with the bread of life.
They thirst not,
  for you give them to drink of the waters
    of your Holy Spirit.
They want not,
  for you are their treasure and wealth.
They dwell in the house of your peace.
(WENGER, pp. 74-75)

Guided Prayer Exercise: Meditative Prayer

One way Christians have "made their home in Christ" is
to enter into the images of Jesus' parables and let them
become part of their prayer. If you want to pray using
Jesus' image of the vine and branches, follow these suggestions. You will need at least fifteen to twenty minutes for
this kind of prayer.

1. Listen to the hymn "Thou true Vine, that heals"
(Hymnal, 373).

2. Quiet your heart and mind by spending a few

moments in silence. Then open yourself to the presence of God's Spirit with a simple prayer: "I open myself to you, God. Let your Spirit guide me into your presence."

3. Imagine a vineyard on a hillside in early morning light. Touch the dew on vines and leaves. Breathe the cool, moist air. Watch a gentle breeze blow across the hillside. Hear the whispering of the leaves. Feel the warmth of the sun's first rays.

4. In your imagination, picture a gardener entering the vineyard. Watch the gardener examine the vines with tender care. See the gardener spade and loosen the soil. Notice the gardener's pride in the healthy vineyard.

5. After a time imagine that rain clouds gather on the horizon. Feel gentle drops of rain falling on the vineyard. Sense the pulse of life and energy as the vine and branches receive moisture and are stirred to new growth.

6. As time passes, imagine that the branches grow stronger and become mature. One day fruit appears, then ripens in the sun, and eventually is harvested. See the joy of the gardener as baskets of plump, juicy grapes are gathered from the vineyard.

7. Remain in silence with the image of the joyful gardener, sturdy vine, and fruitful branches. What do you sense the Spirit is saying to you with these images? How are you being called to receive the life of Jesus, the true Vine? What "moisture" are you receiving? What fruit is growing? Give thanks for God's tender care and life-giving presence.

8. Celebrate God's presence and care as you sing or listen to the hymn "Thou true Vine, that heals."

Martyr's Prayer

Pilgram Marpeck was a mining engineer with the Tyrolean government who became an Anabaptist. One of the few early leaders to escape a martyr's death, he was nevertheless persecuted and forced to leave his home. After he escaped to Strasbourg in 1528, he helped to organize new communities of faith and also wrote extensively about his beliefs and convictions. This prayer is adapted from a quote attributed to Marpeck.

Prayer of Pilgram Marpeck

Gardener God,
  you have planted and protected us by your faithful hand.
Send us the sap of your grace from Christ, the true Vine,
  and make us blossom and bear the fruit of love
    as a sign of your life in us.
Let the sweet fragrance of the shoots you have planted
  give you praise forever and ever. Amen.

(HAAS, p. 129)

"Those who love me will keep my word, and my Father will love them, and we will come to them and make our home with them. Whoever does not love me does not keep my words; and the word that you hear is not mine, but is from the Father who sent me."

"If you abide in me, and my words abide in you, ask for whatever you wish, and it will be done for you."

"If you keep my commandments, you will abide in my love, just as I have kept my Father's commandments and abide in his love."

John 14:23-24; 15:7, 10

3

Delighting
in God's Word

Do you ever find it hard to delight in God's Word? Many of us do.

Sometimes it's a matter of overfull schedules. We want to meditate on Scripture but can't seem to squeeze it into our crowded days. Or we may have early memories of dutifully reading a prescribed number of Bible verses or praying about a long list of needs, but the practice brought little life or joy, so somewhere along the way we dropped the habit of regular meditation and prayer.

Perhaps we lack tools or skills. No one has taught us how to pray or how to come to Scripture with an open heart ready to receive God's Word like a love letter written to us personally. We haven't yet discovered that prayer is a relationship and that the Spirit still breathes life into words written thousands of years ago. For any of these reasons, or perhaps others, we may have lost—or never developed—a love for God's Word.

God's commandments can become a constant source of joy for each of us, just as they were for those of whom the psalmist sang, "Their delight is in the law of the Lord, and on his law they meditate day and night" (Psalm 1:2). These ancient Hebrews were in love with Torah. Not just with words inscribed on stone. Not with precise legal codes. Not even with the passionate poetry of the psalm-singers and prophets. What the people of God cherished above all else was the Word of God, the life-giving revelation of God's own will.

Torah included God's instructions to Moses at Sinai. Torah also came to include the teachings of the prophets—directives for Israel's moral, ethical, and worship life. Because these words were God-given, Israel trusted in their goodness. The giving of Torah, Israel believed, was an act of love, and God's people were called to respond to this loving gift with joyful obedience.

Jesus called his disciples to that same loving obedience when he said, "Those who love me will keep my word." But then he went further. He instructed them not only to obey his commandments but to allow his words to abide in them. Outward observance was not enough. They were to honor all that Jesus honored, love all that Jesus loved, hate all that Jesus hated.

Jesus calls us to embrace the whole of his message—not only his spoken words, but also his life, death, and resurrection. Jesus himself is the message, the Word made flesh. The more completely we allow God's Word to abide in us—God's thoughts becoming our thoughts, God's desires becoming our desires, God's dreams becoming our dreams—the more we will experience the reality of Jesus' promise, "ask for whatever you wish, and it will be done for you." Through us, God's will shall be done.

If we don't have a love for God's Word, how can we develop one?

Ask God for a hunger for the Word. Keep asking—daily, if you remember to—until a strong love for God's Word takes root. Like Torah, the ability to delight in God's Word is a gift.

Make time. Do you have a time and place where you can spend uninterrupted minutes with God each day? Ask God to help you find or create such a time.

Start small. Set realistic, easily reached goals for your meditation time—even five minutes a day. Then as meditation becomes a habit, you can increase the time you spend.

Experiment. Try different ways of reading or meditating on Scripture, like the one following this meditation. Look for books that offer guides for meditation, ask people you know who delight in Scripture what works for them, or experiment with ideas of your own. There is no one right way to meditate on Scripture. Experiment until you find ways that help Scripture come alive for you.

Be patient. Waiting beside a railroad track doesn't cause a train to come, but if you wait long enough, one will come. In the same way, you cannot force the Holy Spirit to speak to you through Scripture, but you can make a habit of listening so that when the Spirit speaks, you hear. This is what you are doing by setting aside daily time for meditation.

If we cut ourselves off from the words of life by not regularly spending time in Scripture, eventually, like branches cut from the vine, we wither and die. But if we abide in Jesus' words, allowing them to shape who we are becoming, we will have the honor of becoming fruitful branches through which he accomplishes his work.

Anabaptist Voices

An intimate acquaintance with God's Word and devotion to its teaching were identifying features of the first Anabaptists. Within the Word the Anabaptists not only found guidance for their lives but a deep, enduring companionship with Jesus Christ. In a colorful image which speaks of the life-giving qualities of Scripture, Menno Simons spoke of Christ Jesus and his blessed Word as "the green, blossoming rod of faith" (WENGER, p. 94). George Blaurock, an effective evangelist among the early Anabaptists, described the divine Word as a gift of pure grace (VAN BRAGHT, p. 431).

In a book called *True Christian Faith*, Menno Simons poured out his praise to God that simple folk—not the learned or powerful—can receive the treasure of the knowledge of God through the Word:

Ah, dear children, you who are born of the Word of the Lord through the Spirit, ponder how incomprehen-

44

sibly great the heavenly goodness and grace have been, which have been manifest unto us through Christ [Jesus].... Recall that [God] has so graciously permitted us to find through His Spirit this great treasure, the true knowledge of the kingdom of God; the treasure which lies buried in the field and has made known to us the mystery of His good pleasure, and the true regenerating knowledge of His holy Gospel which cannot be taught in schools, nor purchased at any price, nor imported from foreign lands, nor earned by any good works. Recall that He has opened to us with the key of His Word and Spirit the saving Truth, and has closed it to all emperors, kings, lords, princes, the wise and the learned ones of the whole world (WENGER, pp. 325-326).

For Anabaptists, it was not enough simply to delight in God's word. Such devotion called forth a way of life which corresponded to Jesus' own life of love. Hans Denck wrote in 1526:

Let him who honors Scripture but is cold in divine love beware lest he make of Scripture an idol, as do all text-educated [scribes] who are not educated for the Kingdom of God (BAUMAN, p. 149).

A year later in 1527 Hans Hut, a fiery preacher and bookseller, echoed Denck's conviction when he wrote:

The Word must be received...with a true heart through the Holy Spirit and become flesh in us. That happens through great terror and trembling as with Mary when she heard the will of God from the angel. The Word must be born in us too.... And where the Word has been born and become flesh in us so that we praise God for such a favor, our heart has found peace and we become Christ's mother, brother and sister (HAAS, p. 274).

Guided Prayer Exercise: Praying the Scripture

For Christians today, delighting in God's Word can happen in many ways. It can happen in Sunday morning worship when we hear God's Word proclaimed or as we sing songs and hymns together. It can happen when the words of a psalm come to mind as we walk along a lakeshore. It can happen in a time set apart each day for meeting God.

One of the most significant ways Christians abide in Christ's words is by meditating on Scripture. An ancient prayer practice of the church called "praying the Scriptures" is a simple but fruitful way to let Jesus' words abide in us and then become living and active in obedient words and deeds.

If you want to pray the Scripture, follow these simple steps:

1. *Prepare for prayer.* Quiet your heart and mind by waiting in silence. You may want to light a candle as a sym-

bol of God's presence. Pray for openness to God's Spirit. Then listen to the hymn "I long for your commandments" (Hymnal, 543).

2. *Read the Scripture.* Pick up the Scripture text and read it in a slow, thoughtful way. You may find it helpful to read the text out loud as a way of focusing your attention. Listen as though God is speaking to you personally.

3. *Meditate on Scripture.* Now read the text again—this time reading slowly until you come to a word, phrase, or sentence that attracts you. Stop reading and remain with the word or phrase, savoring its goodness and sweetness in much the same way that you would delight in well-seasoned food. Listen for the Spirit's voice speaking to you from the text.

If you have a journal, jot down the words or phrases that emerge during this time of meditation. Pay special attention to any images, actions, or feelings that catch your attention. Let your imagination be part of your meditation.

4. *Respond in prayer.* After listening to the Spirit's voice, pray to God silently, out loud, or in writing. Perhaps your response will be in the form of thanksgiving or praise or confession. Perhaps you will be prompted to intercede in prayer for others. Express to God whatever is in your heart.

5. *Remain in God's presence.* After you have listened to God's Word and responded in prayer, wait in silence for a few more moments. Simply rest in God's presence. Receive the gift of peace. Thank God for being with you. Conclude your time of prayer by singing or listening to the hymn "I long for your commandments."

Martyr's Prayer

The letters of Anabaptist believers who suffered in prison were often liberally sprinkled with Scripture quotations. As they awaited death, the believers not only received comfort and courage from meditating on Scripture but admonished their families and sisters and brothers in the faith to abide in God's Word.

When Jerome Segers and his wife, Lijsken Dircks, were imprisoned for their faith and placed in separate cells in the Antwerp, Belgium, prison, Lijsken wrote to Jerome that the prison keepers had asked her, "Why do you trouble yourself with the Scriptures; attend to your sewing" (VAN BRAGHT, p. 515).

In his response, Jerome counseled his wife, "And though they may tell you to attend to your sewing, this does not prevent us; for Christ has called us all, and commanded us to search the Scriptures, since they testify of Him; and Christ also said that Magdalene had chosen the better part, because she searched the Scriptures Matthew 11:28; John 5:39; Luke 10:42" (VAN BRAGHT, p. 516).

Prayer of Jerome Segers

Keep me, O crucified Christ;
 satisfy me with your divine Word,
 feed me with the bread of life and understanding,
 give me to drink the water of wisdom

and the unadulterated milk from the fountain of life.
Keep my soul unto salvation. Amen.

(VAN BRAGHT, p. 517)

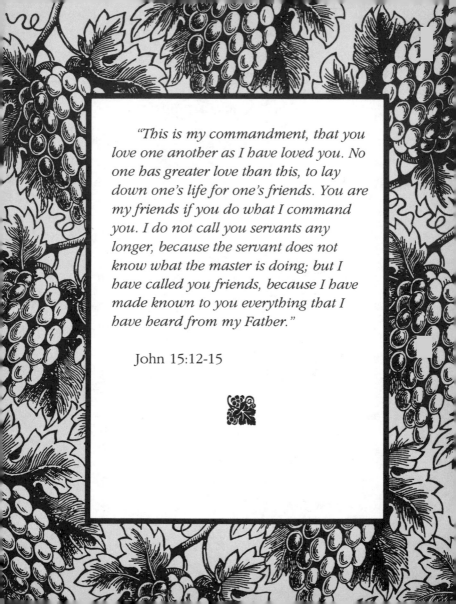

"This is my commandment, that you love one another as I have loved you. No one has greater love than this, to lay down one's life for one's friends. You are my friends if you do what I command you. I do not call you servants any longer, because the servant does not know what the master is doing; but I have called you friends, because I have made known to you everything that I have heard from my Father."

John 15:12-15

4

Becoming Jesus' Friends

IN THE COURTS of Roman emperors and eastern rulers, a highly select group of people were called friends of the court. While most of the ruler's subjects could not even get an appointment to see him, these few could see him any time. They would even come to the ruler's bed chamber at the beginning of the day to counsel him before he met with other governing officials. These friends were intimate with their ruler.

In much the same way, the disciples eventually became intimate with Jesus. Perhaps the highest words of honor Jesus ever spoke to them were, "I do not call you servants any longer...; but I have called you friends." Jesus had already greatly honored these men by calling them to follow and serve him. Moses, Joshua, David, Paul, and others felt honored to be considered servants of God. But with these words Jesus was bestowing an even greater honor.

When Jesus called the disciples friends, what did he

mean? He meant that he could confide in them. "The servant does not know what the master is doing...; but ... I have made known to you everything that I have heard from my Father." Good servants are loyal even if they don't know what their master is doing or why. For three years, the disciples had obeyed Jesus' instructions, sometimes blindly. They had been faithful servants. But with the cross approaching, Jesus wanted them to understand not only what he expected of them but also his hopes, his dreams, his reason for living, so his purposes could become theirs.

Scripture uses several words for friendship. Here Jesus uses a word meaning "loved one" or "dear one." How do we become Jesus' dear ones? Jesus doesn't leave us wondering. "You are my friends," he says, "if you do what I command you." It's that simple. And that hard. We become Jesus' friends through obedience.

That shouldn't surprise us. Suppose, for example, you go to work for a small company and do your assigned work well. The company manager is impressed and before long promotes you to a position with more responsibility. After you serve faithfully a year or two in that role, the manager makes you a member of the executive team that works closely with her to make and implement the decisions that will determine the success or failure of the company. You spend many hours working closely with the manager, and in time her vision for the business becomes more and more your own.

If you have a good relationship with your boss, the day may come when in the middle of a conference she lays her yellow pad on her desk and just starts talking. She lets you see how worried she is about a business problem, in spite of the bold face she puts on in public. Or she describes what a heavy load it is to care for her mother whose health is failing. Or she tells you about a minor victory just because she needs to share her joy with someone.

You have related to your boss as a faithful servant for years. Now, you have become her friend. How can you tell? Because she has confided in you.

And how did you become her friend? Through faithful service you earned her trust. Through time spent with her you came to know her, not just as a supervisor, but as a personal friend.

And that is how we become intimate with God. Through obedient service and time spent, more obedient service and more time spent, we, like the disciples, are eventually welcomed into that honored circle Jesus calls friends.

When you think about it, it's an amazing thing that Jesus invites you and me to be his personal friends. Yet as staggering as the invitation is, we often seem to forget we've ever been invited. Maybe it would help us remember if we looked upon each invitation to the Lord's table as an invitation to deeper communion—a more intimate relationship—with him. That very first Lord's Supper, after all, Jesus shared only with his closest friends, the very same men to whom he said, "I no longer call you servants but friends." Each time we are invited to eat the bread and drink the cup, we are being invited to share in that intimate fellowship.

Incredible as it may seem, Jesus doesn't want us to remain mere subjects who only hear reports about what our faraway leader is doing; he invites us to become "friends of the court" to whom he, our master and our friend, can bare his very soul.

I can't even conceive of any higher honor. Can you?

Anabaptist Voices

Throughout their experiences of testing and persecution, the Anabaptists were sure of one thing: that love is a gift of God. "One thing is certain;..." Hans Denck wrote, "this little spark [of love], however small it may be in a person, does not come from humankind but from the source of Perfect Love" (HAAS, p. 77).

Perhaps they understood Jesus' call to intimate friendship more thoroughly than we do. They had given themselves—body, soul, and spirit—into God's care and keeping. Without a deep sense of God's love, they could not have followed such a demanding and dangerous path. Yet within this committed relationship, they experienced the mystery of living as coheirs with Christ. Denck wrote that even though Christians are not perfect as Christ was, "those who received the Holy Spirit, are in God one with and equal to Christ, so that what pertains to one pertains to the other. As Christ does, so do they also" (HAAS, p. 272).

Another image Anabaptists used to describe the depth of their friendship with Christ is the marriage relationship. In 1530 Melchior Hoffman, a tireless preacher and evangelist, wrote an extended analogy describing the profound intimacy between Christians and their Lord:

> When now the bride of the Lord Jesus Christ has given herself over to the Bridegroom in baptism, which is the sign of the covenant, and has betrothed herself and yielded herself to him of her own free will ... thereupon the Bridegroom and exalted Lord Jesus Christ comes and by his hand ... takes bread (just as a bridegroom takes a ring or a piece of gold) and gives himself to his bride with the bread (just as the bridegroom gives himself to his bride with the ring).... They together are thus one body, one flesh, one spirit and one passion, as bridegroom and bride.
>
> Yea, more. The bride is in truth assured the moment she takes the bread that she has accepted the true Christ for her Lord and Head and eternal Bridegroom in order that ever thereafter his will, spirit, mind and good pleasure may be in her and that she on her part gives herself over unto his will with all her heart, spirit, feeling and will (HAAS, p. 328).

Guided Prayer Exercise: Centering Prayer

People who are truly close friends don't need to spend all their time talking when they are together. After a time of animated conversation—both listening and speaking—they may fall silent. They are comfortable just being together.

Centering prayer is like the quiet, deep communion of

intimate friends who linger at the table after finishing a meal. They do not need words to communicate. They simply enjoy each other's presence. When we enter into prayer that goes beyond words, we may also be given the special gift of a sense of God's nearness.

If you want to experience centering prayer, follow these suggestions:

1. Listen to the hymn "Jesus, priceless treasure" (Hymnal, 595). Close your eyes. Relax your mind and body by taking several deep breaths.

2. Imagine that Jesus is present with you. Perhaps you are facing each other across a table or walking together along a path. How does it feel to be so close to Jesus? Are you comfortable? Uncomfortable?

3. Then imagine that Jesus says to you, "You are my friend, my dearly beloved friend." Hear the words with your heart as well as your mind. Let Jesus keep repeating the phrase, "You are my friend."

4. What response arises within you? Can you accept the gift of Jesus' friendship? Do you want to say anything to Jesus?

5. Wait quietly in silence for a few minutes. Don't say or do anything. If you become distracted or restless, come back to the phrase, "You are my friend." Stay in this receptive mode until you feel at peace and your prayer seems complete.

6. Give thanks to God for calling you to friendship. Rejoice in the gift of intimate communion God offers you.

7. Conclude your time of prayer by singing or listening to the hymn "Jesus, priceless treasure."

Martyr's Prayer

In 1573 Maeyken van Deventer, a pious and God-fearing woman, was imprisoned in Rotterdam, Holland. When she could not be persuaded to turn from her steadfast faith, she was sentenced to die. In a last testament for her children, she expressed her deep desire that they too would become Christ's friends. She wrote, "Go to God; fear Him alone; keep His commandments; remember all His words to do...them; write them upon the tables of your heart, and bind them on your forehead, and speak of His statutes night and day, and you shall be a pleasant branch in the garden of the Lord, yea, a beloved plant growing up in Zion" (VAN BRAGHT, pp. 978-79).

Prayer of Maeyken van Deventer

O holy Father,
  sanctify the children of your handmaiden in your truth,
    and keep them from all evil,
    and from all unrighteousness,
  for your holy name's sake.
O Almighty Father,
  I commend them unto You,
     since they are your creatures;
  care for them,
    for they are your handiwork;
  so that they may walk in your paths. Amen.

(VAN BRAGHT, p. 979)

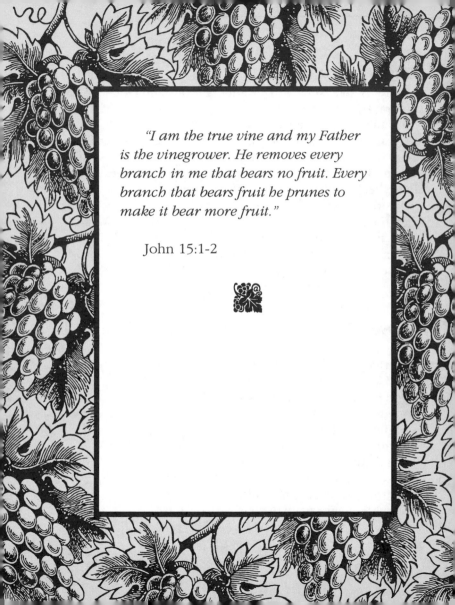

"I am the true vine and my Father is the vinegrower. He removes every branch in me that bears no fruit. Every branch that bears fruit he prunes to make it bear more fruit."

John 15:1-2

5

Pruning for Greater Fruitfulness

HAVE YOU EVER had the satisfaction of knowing God was using you to touch another person's life?

Like that day you visited a friend or relative in the nursing home. When you first got there her spirits were low, but by the time you left she was all smiles.

Maybe you taught Sunday school and after class a student told you how something you said helped her with a problem she was facing.

Or you've watched your own children mature in ways that make you proud to be their parent, and you realize that all the love and time and energy you've poured into their lives has been the best investment you ever made.

This is ministry. This is what Jesus means by bearing fruit.

Few things bring more joy than knowing that through us God's love has touched and changed another person's life. It's only natural then that when the time comes to leave behind a ministry that has given us joy, the parting will not be painless.

You're excited about the new women's ministry God is leading you into, but you also know that to do it justice, you must give up the Sunday school class you've been teaching. Saying good-bye to students you love isn't easy.

Failing eyesight forces you to give up driving so you can no longer visit the nursing home. You know God will show you new ways to serve, but the loss is still hard.

Your last child leaves home so you no longer relate to your children as children, but as adults. New ways of relating bring their own rewards, but that chapter of your life that has brought such joy is closed.

Just as the vine has its growing seasons, our lives and ministries have their seasons. One season of fruitfulness ends and another begins. To prepare to embrace the new, we must first let go of the old, and letting go can be hard.

In the life of the vine, this letting go is called pruning. It seems a brutal reward for a branch that has yielded luscious grapes to cut off six, eight, even ten feet of its luxuriant growth, leaving only a stub of a few inches. What vinegrower would be so merciless? The answer is, any vinegrower who wants to make the branch as fruitful as possible.

As harsh as it may seem, pruning is not punishment; it is actually a tribute to the branch. Unfruitful branches don't get pruned; they're simply cut from the vine and burned. In choosing to prune a branch rather than discard it, the vinegrower is both recognizing its past fruitfulness and expressing faith in its future fruitfulness.

And when the vinegrower comes with a pruning knife, what gets cut away? Weeds? Thorns? Disease? No, the vinegrower cuts away the healthy wood of the branch. Not because it's bad, not because there's anything wrong with it, but because in the coming season the long branch would sap energy needed to grow fruit.

In the Christian life, what is pruned is the long shoot of the previous season's ministry. Though it was produced by the life of the vine itself, it is no longer needed for fruitbearing, so the vinegrower relentlessly cuts it away.

With this image of pruning, Jesus gives us the secret to navigating smoothly the difficult transition between seasons of ministry. If we appreciate the purpose of the pruning—greater fruitfulness—we can choose not to focus on our loss. We can instead give thanks for the privilege we've enjoyed of bearing fruit for the vine in the past season and eagerly anticipate the greater fruitfulness God is preparing us for in the season to come.

You get word that your job—a job you love, a job through which you have served others—will soon end due to layoffs. It is appropriate, of course, to grieve your loss. But then you have a choice. Will you be afraid? Will you despair? Will you become bitter? Or can you see the vinegrower's pruning knife silently at work, bringing to an end one season of ministry to prepare the way for even greater ministry? Can you look forward expectantly to what is to come?

Probably few of us will actually enjoy "being pruned," but if we can see pruning as the vinegrower sees it, perhaps we can at least learn not to resist it. We can cooperate with the vinegrower by gracefully releasing last year's productive growth, knowing this will lead to the even greater joy that comes through even greater fruitfulness.

Anabaptist Voices

Growing to Christian maturity, according to the Anabaptists, was not an automatic process. Although the Christian life begins when we answer the call to follow Christ, our spiritual life expands and deepens as we walk with Christ daily. Menno Simons wrote of this renewal process and its fruit:

> A genuine Christian faith cannot be idle, but it changes, renews, purifies, sanctifies and justifies more and more. It gives peace and joy, for by faith it knows that...sin and death are conquered through Christ, and that grace, mercy, pardon from sin and eternal life are acquired through Him. In full confidence it approaches the Father in the name of Christ, receives the Holy Ghost, becomes partaker of the divine nature and is renewed after the image of Him who created him. It lives out the power of Christ which is in it; all its ways are righteousness, godliness, honesty, truth, wisdom, goodness, kindness, light, love, peace (HAAS, p. 208).

Part of the daily walk with Christ is receiving God's

pruning—that continued shaping which makes our lives and ministries even more fruitful. Yet as necessary and beneficial as pruning is for good health, sometimes we cannot help fearing or resisting its effects. Hans Denck recognized this tendency and encouraged the followers of Christ not to forget who the Pruner is:

That you, however, seek yourself and not God for his own sake you demonstrate...in that you perpetually seek a hiding place in order that you might escape the hand of God. For you, being a desolate little blade of grass and he an immeasurably great rock, are always anxious that he will crush you if you silently yield to him. For so it appears to flesh and blood before a person offers himself up. Where he seeks salvation, there appears to be damnation. That does not appeal to the taste of perverted nature. If [a person] would but hold still, there would be time and place for the spirit of the lamb to bear witness and declare that this is the singular way to blessedness, namely, losing one's self. For, since God and all his works are the very best, therefore his breaking, which is so contrary to our nature, must necessarily be infinitely better than all that happens in heaven, on, and under the earth (BAUMAN, p. 89).

Guided Prayer Exercise: Prayer as Dialogue

Because prayer is a relationship, it often involves a dialogue between ourselves and God. We speak our concerns or questions to God, and we wait for God's response. Sometimes we hear a word from God very clearly; at other times we may dimly sense a direction or a correction that is needed. Prayer as dialogue means opening ourselves to ongoing interaction in which we receive guidance and are continually renewed by the cleansing, healing action of the Spirit.

To enter into prayer as dialogue, follow these suggested steps:

1. Listen to the hymn "Open, Lord, my inward ear" (Hymnal, 140).

2. Quiet your heart and mind by waiting in silence for a few moments. Invite Jesus to be present as your partner in dialogue.

3. Reflect on the good fruit God has brought forth in your life. Think about attitudes, relationships, areas of ministry, and daily actions; You may want to write your reflections in a list. Give thanks for the Spirit's creative, renewing work within you.

4. Ask Jesus to show you what other fruit is desired in your life. Wait and listen for a response. Are you aware of God's pruning action? Is there something you are being asked to let go? Are you resisting or afraid of changes which may be required? Express those fears or concerns to Jesus. Listen for a response. Give thanks for God's faith-

ful, nurturing attention.

5. Close your time of prayer by singing or listening to the hymn "Open, Lord, my inward ear."

Matyr's Prayer

Maeyken Boosers, mother of several children, was imprisoned for her faith at Doornick in Belgium. During her imprisonment she wrote letters to her father and mother and children as well as to sisters and brothers in the church. In one letter she describes her interrogation by local officials and mentions that she was baptized at age twenty-three or twenty-four years. When she would not give information about other believers, she was bound and tortured on the rack.

Later after further questioning, Maeyken refused to give up her beliefs regarding baptism and was burned to ashes on September 18, 1564. Throughout her letters is a strongly expressed desire to remain true to the faith to which she had been called. This prayer is adapted from a quote attributed to Maeyken Boosers.

Prayer of Maeyken Boosers

O Lord,
   my heart constantly longs to be fit in your sight
      that I might finish to your praise
         that which you have commenced in me. Amen.
                              (Van Braght, p. 667)

PART 2

Joined in Love

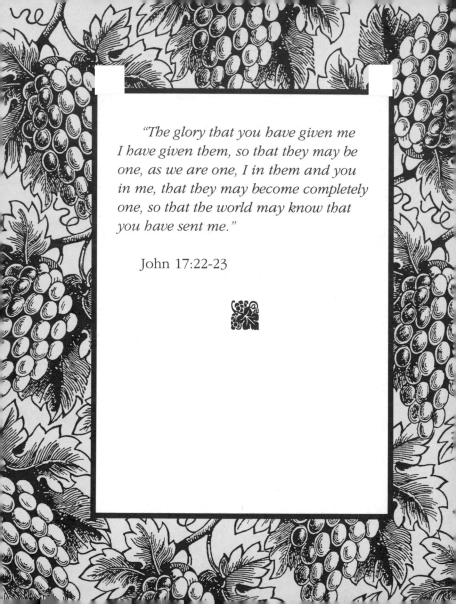

"*The glory that you have given me I have given them, so that they may be one, as we are one, I in them and you in me, that they may become completely one, so that the world may know that you have sent me.*"

John 17:22-23

6

Joined by the Life of the Vine

Hᴀᴠᴇ ʏᴏᴜ ᴇᴠᴇʀ been surrounded by hundreds or even thousands of people—perhaps at a conference or at an airport or on the streets of an unfamiliar city—and still felt lonely? We can feel lonely in a crowd because loneliness seldom comes from being alone; it comes from not being connected with others in ways that make us feel safe, understood, and cared for.

Gospel songs and choruses with lyrics like "How can I be lonely?" and "Jesus is all I need" suggest that friendship with God fully meets this need. And perhaps there are a few hermit saints somewhere whose need for companionship is fully met through communion with God alone.

But that doesn't seem to be true for most of us. Why not? Is it because we're so spiritually immature that we have to rely on the "crutch" of other people? No, it's because God made us this way.

After creating Adam, God looked the situation over and

said, "It is not good that the man should be alone" (Gen. 2:18). Adam already had fellowship with God—a fellowship still unmarred by sin—but it wasn't enough. Adam still needed human companionship. So God created Eve, and Adam and Eve enjoyed each other's company.

Then Adam and Eve sinned, estranging themselves not only from God, but also from each other. Because their rebellion has been repeated in every generation since, today we live in a world of widespread fear and loneliness, a world where billions of people are alienated from God and each other.

But, fortunately, sin doesn't have the last word. The gift of community God gave in the beginning, the gift we threw away, God continues to offer anew. The writer of 1 John extends an invitation: "What we have seen and heard we declare to you, so that you and we together may share in a common life, that life which we share with the Father and his Son Jesus Christ" (1 John 1:3, NEB). We are invited to enter into community both with God and each other.

And what is it that binds this community together? Personal attraction? Shared culture? National loyalties? Doctrinal agreement?

No, this is a community formed by the life—the divine life—its members share. Or, to use the imagery of the vine and the branches, this is a community made up of the vine and all the branches through which the life of the vine flows. Not only is each branch connected to the vine, but through the vine, all the branches are joined to one another. Sometimes we may not be sure if this is good news or bad. However appealing the idea of community may be, in practice, living in community is often messy and always hard work. Wouldn't it be nice, we may wonder, if we could just enjoy God without having to bother with all the brothers and sisters in God's family?

But God doesn't give us that option. To enter into relationship with God is to join the family of God, which includes people hard to get along with, people whose politics annoy us, people whose customs baffle us, and people whose words or actions embarrass us. How can God possibly expect us to relate meaningfully with people with whom we have nothing in common except our faith in God?

Well, that is not only the mystery of Christian community but also its genius. Christian community doesn't depend on human affinity of any stripe—cultural, political, or doctrinal. God's life flowing through us as the life of the vine coarses through its branches—this and nothing else makes us one in Christ.

While I must stretch to include those with whom I would not naturally choose to associate, I also take comfort in knowing that others will stretch to include me. When I am hard to get along with, I have brothers and sisters who will not desert me. When my views seem strange or wrongheaded, they will still love me. When I make choices that leave them shaking their heads, they will not disown me. We are bound together by something that runs deeper than our likes and dislikes, our similarities and dissimilarities, our agreements and disagreements. We are joined by a reality that empowers us to transcend our differences enough to truly love one another.

The Christian community does not always live up to this high calling, it's true. Yet it is only here that we can ever find a fully satisfying and lasting answer to our own hunger to be safe, understood, and cared for—in the shared life created by the divine life we share.

Anabaptist Voices

The Anabaptists taught that the church is a visible community of faith. Though they also understood the church to be an invisible union, they emphasized its earthy, human character. The church is a body of people—a community—who care for each other and live as Christ's followers in the world.

In 1542 Peter Riedemann, a teacher and theologian who was often jailed for his beliefs, described the visible church as "a lantern of righteousness, in which the light of grace is borne and held before the whole world.... The church ... is filled with the light of Christ as a lantern is illuminated and made bright by the light ... to give light to others still walking in darkness" (KLAASSEN, p. 112).

The Anabaptists also understood that the unity of the body cannot be created by human ingenuity. Community is a gift from God offered to all who enter the church through baptism. It did not matter what people's pasts had been; when they were baptized they were welcomed into Christ's family. Pilgram Marpeck wrote in 1531, "I pray

God my heavenly Father that He will not allow me to be separated from such a gathering and fellowship of the Holy Spirit; it makes no difference who they are or where they gather in the whole world. I hope to be in their fellowship and to submit myself to the rule of the Holy Spirit of Christ in the obedience of faith" (HAAS, p. 167).

The unique character of the church and its ongoing life were dependent on the Spirit's transforming power. Menno Simons described the church as "God's elect, His saints and beloved...who are in Christ and He in them; who hear and believe His Word.... For all who are in Christ are new creatures, flesh of His flesh, bone of His bone, and members of His body" (WENGER, p. 402).

Guided Prayer Exercise: Prayer of Intercession

Just as Jesus prayed for the protection and unity of the church (see John 17), so too Christians today are called to pray for the health and unity of the church. If you want to pray a prayer of intercession on behalf of the church, follow these steps:

1. Listen to the hymn "All praise to our redeeming Lord" (Hymnal, 21).

2. Enter into a few moments of silence. As you wait before God, call to mind those in your congregation who are closest to you—the people who love and support you. Imagine them standing before God, shining with the light of Christ's glory. Ask God to bless them and make them a blessing.

3. Then bring to mind those in your congregation whom you know less well or those with whom you've experienced disagreements or conflicts. Imagine them also standing before God, shining with the light of Christ's glory. Ask God to bless them and make them a blessing.

4. Imagine your entire congregation shining as a "lantern of righteousness" in the world. Ask God to protect your church, to make you one in Christ, and to make your ministries fruitful in bringing many people to Christ.

5. Finally, imagine Christ's church throughout the world as a beacon of light bringing hope with the good news of Jesus Christ. Ask God to bless the church and make it a blessing.

6. Close your time of prayer by singing or listening to the hymn "All praise to our redeeming Lord."

Martyr's Prayer

Among the colorful early leaders in the Anabaptist movement was Jakob Hutter, a Tyrolean minister sent to Moravia. Though the Moravian Anabaptists enjoyed religious freedom for a short time, eventually they too were persecuted for their faith. Jakob returned to his native land where he hid in the cellars of his friends' homes, in forests, in secret places in the hills, and attempted to continue preaching to small groups of believers. Eventually he was apprehended, imprisoned, and tortured for several months near Innsbruck. He was burned at the stake in the early spring of 1536.

In a poetic description of the church as God's garden, Hutter described his Christian sisters and brothers as "growing in godly righteousness and flourishing like lovely tulips and sweet-scented lilies. As a garden bursts into leaf and flower after rain in May, so they are budding and blossoming in God's sight, flourishing in the fear of God and in His love and peace.... They are a joy to my heart and deserve the name 'garden of the Lord,' as Scripture says. For them I praise and thank God with all my heart" (HAAS, p. 160). This prayer is adapted from the writings of Jakob Hutter.

Prayer of Jakob Hutter

O living God,
   pour heavenly blessings upon the Church, your garden.
 Water your garden with rain from heaven,
   the comfort of your Holy Spirit
   and the oil of your compassion.
 Protect your garden with a fence to guard it from
   wild beasts;
 Protect it from thunderstorms and from evil blights
   so that its fruit may ripen unto many good works.
 Keep watch until your garden comes to full bloom,
   and bring it to a bountiful harvest. Amen.
                    (HAAS, p. 160)

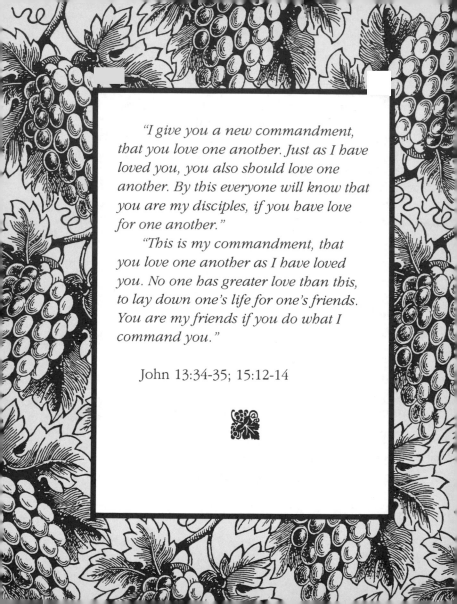

"I give you a new commandment,
that you love one another. Just as I have
loved you, you also should love one
another. By this everyone will know that
you are my disciples, if you have love
for one another."

"This is my commandment, that
you love one another as I have loved
you. No one has greater love than this,
to lay down one's life for one's friends.
You are my friends if you do what I
command you."

John 13:34-35; 15:12-14

7

Joined by Sacrificial Love

Have you ever had a brush with death? Perhaps a serious illness or an accident or near accident that, if things had happened just a bit differently, could have cost you your life?

Such experiences often show us just how much we want to live. This clinging to life is among the most basic of all human instincts. It's a wonderful gift, one that has saved many a person from a premature grave.

Because we've all felt this strong urge to protect our own lives, we may be puzzled when Jesus says, "Those who want to save their life will lose it, and those who lose their life for my sake will find it" (Matt. 16:25). God creates us with an instinct for self-protection, then says that if we try to protect ourselves we'll end up losing our lives? And that we can find life only by giving up our lives? How can this be?

We find a clue in Jesus' words: "I give you a new commandment, that you love one another. As I have loved you, you also should love one another." The law of love was nothing new, of course. Leviticus 19:18 said: "Love your neighbor as yourself." But Jesus was calling his disciples to a new standard of love—not only to love their neighbors as themselves but to love as he loved.

And how was that? "No one has greater love than this, to lay down one's life for one's friends," Jesus said, then stretched out his arms and died, defining once and for all the meaning of his new command. By his life and death, Jesus demonstrated that love for another can be stronger than our instinct for self-preservation.

We admire such love. A father charges into traffic to push his young son out of the path of an oncoming car, knowing full well he is risking his life. A mother rushes into a burning building to rescue her trapped infant. A husband, without hesitation, agrees to donate a kidney so his wife can live.

Sometimes, though, being willing to risk death for another, as heroic as that is, is less difficult than laying down our lives in smaller sacrifices day after day. The father who risks his life to push his son out of a car's path may keep putting off the fishing trip he's promised him. The mother who plunges into a burning building may be reluctant to interrupt her work to comfort her crying baby. The husband who gladly gave his kidney may refuse to turn off Monday-night football long enough to find out what's going on in his wife's life.

To a culture obsessed with looking out for number one, sacrificial love may sound like quaint asceticism or even a wimpish cop-out for those not up to "playing hardball."

But Jesus' warning remains clear. Those devoted to protecting and advancing their own interests will lose their souls. They may keep walking about with smiles on their faces, but inside they can only be empty and dead.

Only those in whom love rises above the instincts of fear and ambition can find real life. Setting aside our own convenience, our own tastes, our own preferences out of a desire to serve another may feel like death, but it is actually the path to life. And, ironic as it seems, living in constant readiness to die for Christian sisters and brothers whom we love is also life-giving, a reality not lost on the early Anabaptists.

In the Lord's Supper, Balthasar Hubmaier saw not only a reminder of Jesus' sacrificial love for us but a renewal of the covenant among members of Christ's body to love one another as he loved us. "What is the Lord's Supper? It is a public token and testimony of love in which one brother pledges himself to another before the church. Just as they are now breaking bread and eating with one another and sharing the cup, so each will offer up body and blood for the other relying on the power of our Lord Jesus Christ" (KLAASSEN, p. 194).

In an age of martyrdom, there were no doubt onlookers who considered the early Anabaptists reckless courters of death. But the vitality of their faith, individually and as a community, proved once again what had earlier been demonstrated by the church of Acts and by various Christian communities through the intervening centuries. In the end, being controlled by the instinct for self-preservation brings death. Only sacrificial love—laying down our lives for one another as Jesus did for us—gives life.

Anabaptist Voices

Michael Sattler, a Benedictine prior who became an Anabaptist, came straight to the point: "Dear fellow members in Christ, you should be admonished not to forget love, without which it is not possible that you be a Christian congregation" (KLAASSEN, p. 103).

The distinguishing mark of the Anabaptists was their sincere love for each other and their willingness, if necessary, to give their lives for their sisters and brothers. Hunted and persecuted by civil and religious authorities, they trusted each other with their possessions and even their children. More than one martyr left children behind in the care of the congregation.

Klaus Felbinger expressed his delight in the love of God's people when he wrote:

Nowhere is a sincere believer happier than in the presence of ... fellow believers. They show each other love, reverence and faithfulness and do good to each other. It is the divine nature of love that makes us feel we are in our neighbor's debt and urges us to serve [them] joyfully wherever we can. Brothers and sisters refresh each other by sharing the gifts God put into their hearts for the good of the Body of Christ, His holy Church, which is the gathering of all the believers who have made a common bond in God's love. And God still has such a Church on earth, that gathering of those who live and work in true community, sharing all blessings of the Spirit and all temporal goods. God wants His children to be like Him, not false but ruled by His Holy Spirit, who gathered them and therefore keeps them as one (HAAS, p. 192).

Celebrating the Lord's Supper was a special sign of love among the Anabaptists. Menno Simons called such occasions a "delightful assembly and Christian marriage feast ... where the hungry consciences are fed with the heavenly bread of the divine Word, with the wine of the Holy Ghost, and where the peaceful, joyous souls sing and play before the Lord" (HAAS, p. 329). In a similar vein, Dirk Philips, a Dutch Anabaptist leader and associate of Menno Simons, wrote:

That is ... a marvelous and blessed union that all Christians are one body and bread in Christ Jesus. They are one bread from the good seed which the heavenly Father has sown in the field of this world. Baked through the fire of love, they are one body of many members of Christ; baptized through one Spirit into one body, and must, according to the example of the natural body, be of one heart and soul and serve each other, be helpful and comforting, just as the members of the natural body do (HAAS, pp. 158-159).

Guided Prayer Exercise: Prayer of Confession

Even though the church is created in love and called to live in love, the people of God sometimes fail to live up to their heritage and calling. Individual congregations fail; so do individuals within the church. At such times, prayers of confession are necessary for cleansing, healing, and the emergence of new life.

If you want to pray a prayer of confession on behalf of yourself and the church, follow these steps:

1. Listen to the hymn "Like the murmur of the dove's song" (Hymnal, 29).

2. Quiet yourself by repeating the final phrase of the hymn "Come, Holy Spirit, come." Contemplate the depth of God's love shown in Jesus Christ to the church and to you as an individual (you may want to reread the Scripture printed at the beginning of this session). Give thanks for all you have received through Christ.

3. Remember the gifts of love you have received through the body of Christ. Give thanks for all these gifts.

4. Ask the Spirit to bring to mind those failures of love in which you or your congregation have taken part. Confess your sin and the sin of your people. Ask God to forgive you. As in Isaiah's vision, imagine God's cleansing as a live coal that touches your lips and body as well as your congregation. Receive the words of grace, "your sin is blotted out" (Isaiah 6:7).

5. In silence, wait before God. Is God asking you to take

some healing or reconciling action? How are you being called to respond?

6. Conclude your time of prayer by singing or listening to the hymn "Like the murmur of the dove's song."

Martyr's Prayer

Tijs Jeuriaenss, a minister of the Word in North Holland, was imprisoned for his faith for over a year. During his imprisonment he wrote many letters to console the believers and prayed for their fellowship and unity. This prayer is adapted from his writings.

In 1569 Minister Tijs was strangled and burned at the stake. His body was then placed outside the dyke in the reeds as food for the birds.

Prayer of Tijs Jeuriaenss

Loving God,
  you have baptized us into one body
    and made us to drink the one Spirit.
Now grant us pure and faithful hearts
    that we may serve one another diligently in love
    and find no cause to separate or divide.
Call each of us to esteem others better than ourselves
      so we may remain together in peace and joy.
Grant these mercies to us and all your people. Amen.
                              (VAN BRAGHT, p. 826)

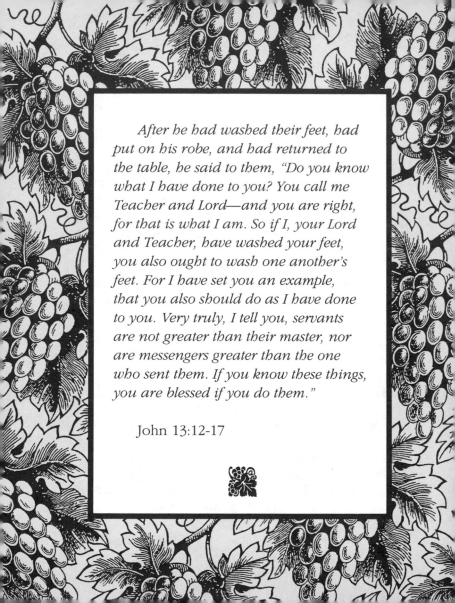

After he had washed their feet, had put on his robe, and had returned to the table, he said to them, "Do you know what I have done to you? You call me Teacher and Lord—and you are right, for that is what I am. So if I, your Lord and Teacher, have washed your feet, you also ought to wash one another's feet. For I have set you an example, that you also should do as I have done to you. Very truly, I tell you, servants are not greater than their master, nor are messengers greater than the one who sent them. If you know these things, you are blessed if you do them."

John 13:12-17

8

Joined Through
Serving One Another

THE STORY of Jesus' washing his disciples' feet doesn't exactly paint a flattering picture of the twelve, so it's easy for us to wag our heads knowingly at what jcrks they were. But I wonder. If I had been there, would I have done any better?

For instance, we cluck at the disciples for thinking themselves too good to wash feet, but it never would have crossed my mind to volunteer to do a slave girl's job. If Jesus had asked me to wash feet, I'd have done it, of course, but I never would have thought of it on my own.

And when the argument broke out about which disciple was the greatest (Luke 22:24), I probably wouldn't have started chanting, "I'm number one!" But I might have joined the fray to cut down to size some bigmouthed disciple campaigning for "top disciple" honors. I might have even silently looked around the table, comparing myself with the other eleven. In light of their glaring faults, chances are it wouldn't have been hard to rank myself "above average."

Then when Jesus took off his robe and stooped to wash feet, I might not have blurted a protest as Peter did, but I wouldn't have been any more at ease with what Jesus was doing.

And when Jesus said, "You also ought to wash one another's feet," I would have been left just as off balance as the rest. What was that supposed to mean?

The truth is, left to my instincts, I'm not any more inclined to be a servant or to let someone else be my servant than the twelve. This servanthood stuff doesn't come naturally to me. Far from it.

That's partly because of human nature, I suppose, and partly because we belong to a culture that worships independence. We're determined to be strong and self-sufficient, and we expect the same of others.

Oh, we're glad to "provide services" to others—accounting services, landscaping services, medical services—depending on our line of work, but something about "being a servant" sounds undignified, inferior, perhaps even inconsistent with self-respect. And while we're glad to employ the "services" of others, we don't really want them to be our servants. We want them to do good work, to be polite and honest—that's all part of the bargain. But if they go much beyond that, it may feel too much like charity, and we don't want that. Don't they know we can take care of ourselves?

The problem with this culture of self-sufficiency is that

it's built on a gigantic lie. No one is or ever can be self-sufficient. Why not? Because our Creator specifically designed us to need each other—so that "the eye cannot say to the hand, 'I have no need of you,' nor again the head to the feet, 'I have no need of you'" (1 Corinthians 12:21).

God didn't create us for independence, but for interdependence. Only as we joyfully serve others and graciously allow others to serve us can society function as God intended.

Obeying Jesus' command to "wash one another's feet" demands more than a nodding acknowledgment of the goodness of service. It calls for challenging our society's idolatry of independence by actively seeking ways to move beyond "providing services" to being a servant. It calls for taking off our masks of self-sufficiency and letting others serve us.

For example, rather than working in my garden while you shingle your garage, I may help you shingle your garage, then let you help me with my garden. Whether this arrangement is any more efficient (it may or may not be, depending on our skills), it serves an important purpose—building relationships. Nor is mutual service a barter arrangement. Servanthood means I help you when you need it and you help me when I need it without either of us needing to keep score.

We need to get beyond the habit of seeing ourselves as either haves and have-nots, strong or weak, givers or receivers. We need to learn instead to take delight in both serving and being served. As we serve each other, our love for one another is not only demonstrated but deepened, and we enjoy more of the shalom God intends for us.

Not to mention that a watching world will sit up and take notice that we are indeed Jesus' disciples.

Anabaptist Voices

One way the Anabaptists expressed their desire and willingness to serve one another was through the practice of washing each other's feet. They literally followed Jesus' command, "If I, your Lord and Teacher, have washed your feet, you also ought to wash one another's feet" (John 13:14).

Pilgram Marpeck saw in Jesus' action a union of the physical and spiritual which is a model for all of Jesus' followers. He wrote in 1542:

> The Lord, when He was gathered with His own in the evening meal, proceeded quite corporally and lovingly with both works as well as words. He stopped at nothing to demonstrate His great love ... through service. It was inadequate for the Lord to address His followers with physical words, consoling and encouraging them, or even to indicate His willingness to give His life for them. Rather, He lowered Himself to washing the feet of His disciples. If we intend to preserve the Lord's Supper correctly, it is vital that we, by loving each other, diligently study and seriously follow the example of our Master (HAAS, p. 109).

Menno Simons carried Jesus' admonition even further and instructed the believers to show their love by washing one another's feet not only in the ritual of the Lord's Supper but in daily life. He said, "Do wash the feet of your beloved brethren and sisters who are come to you from a distance, tired. Be not ashamed to do the work of the Lord, but humble yourselves with Christ, before your brethren, so that all humility of godly quality may be found in you" (WENGER, p. 417).

Guided Prayer Exercise: Praying the Story

It may be easy for us to try to escape the implications of Jesus' call to humble service. Such behavior seems oddly out-of-date or overly literal. One way to enter more fully into the gospel story and personally hear Jesus' call is to pray the story by imaginatively becoming part of the action.

If you want to pray the gospel story by using your imagination, follow these steps:

1. Listen to the hymn "Jesus took a towel" (Hymnal, 449).

2. Read John 13 slowly several times. Then close your eyes and imagine yourself seated at the Passover table with Jesus and his disciples. Visualize the room, the food on the table, candles or oil lamps burning, and the colors and textures of clothing. How do you feel being present with Jesus and his friends? Do you feel at home? Out of place?

3. After the meal, watch Jesus get up from the table, take off his outer robe, tie a towel around his waist, pour water from a basin, and stoop to wash the disciples' feet.

See him wipe their feet with the towel. Notice their expressions and postures.

4. Imagine that Jesus comes to wash your feet. See him kneel before you. Feel the water being poured over your feet. Imagine the touch of Jesus' hands on your feet and the rough texture of the towel as he wipes them dry. Especially notice Jesus' eyes. What is he communicating to you? How do you respond? Do you want to say anything? Do anything?

5. Listen to Jesus' words as though they are spoken to you, "If I, your Lord and Teacher, have washed your feet, you also ought to wash one another's feet." What is your response?

6. If you want to continue praying the gospel story, imagine that someone in your congregation who is not your friend sits in the circle of disciples. See yourself kneel before that person, pour water over his or her feet, and wipe them with a towel. How does this act of humble service make you feel? What do you want to communicate by this action? How does the person respond?

7. Conclude your prayer by singing or listening to the hymn "Jesus took a towel."

Martyr's Prayer

In the late 1520s, seven men, including a lad of fourteen, were confined for a year in a tower in Swabia, Germany. Though they were often threatened and harassed for their faith, they remained faithful. Together they praised God and comforted one another.

When their death sentence was read, they were told that if they would recant, they could return home to their wives and children. The prisoners replied, "We have committed our wives and children to God, who is well able to preserve them; hence cease these words; for we are willing and ready to die." Even a nobleman's last-minute plea to the young teenager could not convince him to give up his faith.

All seven died by the sword and remained faithful witnesses of Jesus Christ.

While they were still in prison, each wrote a prayer and sent it to the believers. What follows is the prayer of one of the seven.

Prayer of the Fifth Martyr

O God,
    you have received us in grace
    and made us your ministers.
  Through your divine assistance
    we have also willingly fulfilled your ministry
      in our weakness.
  Preserve us still further firm in your Word;
    we desire to obey you.
  Come to our aid
    and be our Comforter. Amen.
                   (VAN BRAGHT, p. 434)

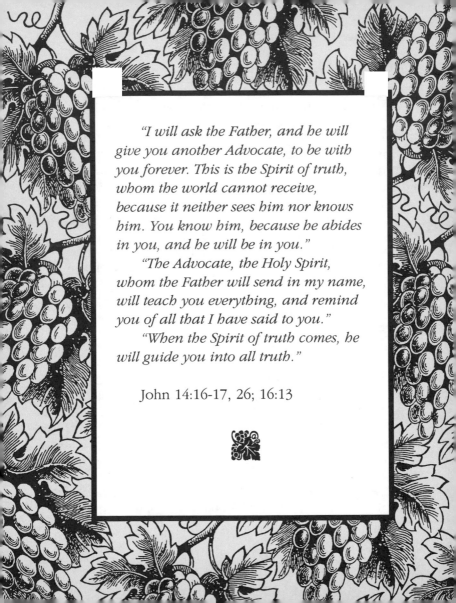

"I will ask the Father, and he will give you another Advocate, to be with you forever. This is the Spirit of truth, whom the world cannot receive, because it neither sees him nor knows him. You know him, because he abides in you, and he will be in you."

"The Advocate, the Holy Spirit, whom the Father will send in my name, will teach you everything, and remind you of all that I have said to you."

"When the Spirit of truth comes, he will guide you into all truth."

John 14:16-17, 26; 16:13

9

Joined in Discerning God's Will

DID YOU EVER get lost in an unfamiliar city? Perhaps you drove around a bit, watching for a sign or landmark to help you get your bearings. If someone in the car knew the neighborhood, you probably asked for his or her advice. If not, you may have pulled out a map and studied it or stopped and asked for directions. When you're lost, you need guidance.

When Jesus told his disciples he was leaving them, they felt lost. They'd spent three years looking to him for vision, for purpose, even for direction in their daily activities. Sure, they'd learned a lot, but when the heat was on, they often reverted to their old ways. They weren't ready to go it alone. They knew it and so did Jesus.

None of us is wise enough to go it alone either. When we've lost our way or we're wrestling with weighty decisions, we too need guidance. And we need it not only during major crises but also for the hundreds of daily decisions that together set the direction of our lives. Without it, we're sure to end up lost.

For those who recognize that they need God's guidance, one of life's biggest questions is "How can I know God's will?" To direct us, God gives us a *map, fellow travelers*, and a *guide*.

The Scriptures are our map. God's will is always consistent with the character of God and the life and teachings of Jesus as revealed in Scripture. Yet, just as a map doesn't do us any good unless we use it, God can only guide us through Scripture if we study it and apply it to our lives.

In *the Christian community* we find fellow travelers. Many who have "been in the neighborhood before" have valuable wisdom to share from their own experience. But guidance through the community goes beyond this. Because we are called to a life together, God calls us to discern guidance for many decisions not individually but in community—a spiritual discipline that goes against the grain of our individualistic culture.

A young professional artist was considering setting aside his art in favor of a job with a steadier cash flow. When he submitted his decision to his church small group, however, the group said, "No, you can't do that. That's the gift God has given you, and you've got to exercise it." Then they backed up their words with action, pooling their funds to create a savings account from which the artist could draw as needed to even out his cash flow. Alone, he would have decided to change jobs. In community, he was encouraged and enabled to continue developing his gift.

The Holy Spirit is our guide. Jesus promised to send his disciples a guide to remind them of everything he had taught them and to keep teaching them, guiding them into "all the truth." This guide was the Holy Spirit who would always be available to them.

And to us. Like the lost traveler, we can stop and ask for directions any time we need them. But for the guide to do us any good, we have to stop, ask, and listen.

It's easy to go through much of life as though we know what's best. Even when we know we need God's guidance, we may do a lot of talking to God but not stop talking long enough to hear an answer. To hear the Spirit, we must cultivate the habit of listening.

Not only do we have to listen; we must also be able to understand what we hear. Not everyone does, you know.

Suppose, for example, that the unfamiliar city where you're lost is Brasilia. When you pull into a service station to ask directions, the attendant speaks only Portuguese. He gives you instructions, but with your tourist-handbook Portuguese, you miss most of what he's saying.

Learning to listen to God can be like that. God is saying something; we're just not sure what.

If I'm having trouble understanding Portuguese, I can get a language tutor. But what if I'm having trouble knowing God's will?

Many have found it helpful to work with a spiritual director. In regular meetings, a spiritual director helps a person reflect on and interpret what God is doing and saying.

Spiritual friends are two people who serve as spiritual

directors for each other, *fellow travelers* who help each other read the map and interpret the voice of the *guide*.

Stopping to hear the whisperings of the Spirit, searching and applying the Scriptures, listening for what God is saying through the Christian community—even these don't guarantee all our decisions will be right. After all, even veteran truck drivers occasionally make wrong turns.

But it sure beats striking out into the unknown alone.

Anabaptist Voices

The Anabaptists believed that it was possible to know and do God's will. Three conversation partners—Scripture, the Christian community, and the Holy Spirit—were required participants in any decision-making process.

Today it is hard to comprehend what a revolutionary practice it was for discernment to belong to laypeople as well as to the clergy. Believing that simple, unlearned people could understand and interpret God's Word, the Anabaptists were not willing to surrender the responsibility of biblical interpretation to scholars or church authorities alone. The prerequisite for faithful interpretation was the same for all people—the fear of the Lord, which is the beginning of wisdom. In 1534, Bernhard Rothmann, a theologian, wrote:

Whoever believes, comes to the right understanding.
He will grasp God's will through faith and carry it out
in deed.... Thus God has restored the Scriptures among

us. In them his will is abundantly known to us and we will adhere to them alone. And if we, with constant diligence, earnestly do what we understand we will daily be taught further by God (KLAASSEN, p. 150).

But Scripture alone was not a sufficient guide. The Holy Spirit was also experienced as an active presence, a divine teacher who would point the way to truth. Jesus had said, "I will not leave you orphans; I will send you the Spirit." In the Twelve Articles of 1526-1527, Balthasar Hubmaier testified, "I believe in the Holy Spirit.... In him I place all my trust that he will teach me all truth" (KLAASSEN, p. 74). The Spirit was specifically experienced as the illuminator of Scripture. Peter Riedemann wrote, "The breath, wind and spirit of God makes the word living and active within us and leads us into all truth" (KLAASSEN, p. 78).

The third partner in the active process of discerning God's will was the congregation itself, the people of God in whom dwelt the living Spirit of the risen Christ. Each member had a personal responsibility to engage in open, honest conversation with other members of the body and become a channel through whom the Holy Spirit might speak. Menno Simons encouraged the believers in 1541:

I beseech you as my sincerely beloved brethren, by the grace of God ... diligently to observe each other unto salvation, in all becoming ways teaching, instructing, admonishing, reproving, warning, and consoling each other as occasion requires, not otherwise than in accordance with the Word of God and in unfeigned love, until we increase in God and become united in faith and in the knowledge of the Son of God, into one perfect [humanity] and according to the measure of the gift of Jesus Christ" (KLAASSEN, p. 218).

The goal of spiritual discernment was not simply to know God's will but to do it. Following Christ's way in the world was the test of all spiritual exercises. With the support of a faithful community of believers, with study of Scripture, and with the guidance of the Holy Spirit, no Christian needed to be left confused or wandering in an uncertain direction.

Guided Prayer Exercise: Prayer of Discernment

Christians face many ordinary, everyday decisions—which school to attend, which job to take, whom to marry or not to marry, how to train and nurture children, how much money to save and how much to give away, or how to respond to changing social and cultural practices. Not all of these everyday decisions can be resolved simply by reading Scripture. Along with knowing and understanding Scripture, we are dependent on the illumination of the Holy Spirit and the counsel of other Christians for guidance.

Perhaps one of the most overlooked resources for discernment is the practice of silence. Throughout the history of the church, Christians have spent time in solitary prayer when they faced perplexing decisions. Sometimes, in the midst of silence, they also met with a spiritual guide or director who helped them discern God's leading more clearly.

The next time your congregation or small group faces an important decision, you may want to try the following approach to discernment.

1. Listen to the hymn "Christ from whom all blessings" (Hymnal, 365).

2. Invite the presence of God's Spirit to illuminate the group's process of decision making.

3. State the problem as clearly as possible. Ask several people to offer various solutions to the problem, incorporating biblical perspectives and any other pertinent information.

4. Allow time for questions of clarification. Do not debate the issues at this point. Simply focus on information.

5. Ask everyone to spend a period of time in silence—fifteen or twenty minutes, depending upon the time available. Invite them to pray for clearer perspectives and a sense of God's leading. Participants may want to jot down thoughts, feelings, observations, or Scriptures they become aware of during the silence.

6. Reconvene the group and invite people to reflect on their experience of silence. What did they become aware of? What questions do they have now? Is more information needed? Have all perspectives been clearly heard? Is more

time needed for discussion? Has a common sense of direction begun to emerge?

7. If a sense of direction is emerging, describe the option as clearly as possible. Again invite participants to spend a brief period of time in silence—perhaps five to ten minutes. Ask them to pray for confirmation of God's leading.

8. Gather the group again and ask for further reflections. If the direction which emerged earlier is confirmed, offer a prayer of thanksgiving and ask for the Spirit's continued guidance. If no common direction has emerged, discuss what additional steps are needed and pray together for further guidance.

9. Close by singing or listening to the hymn "Christ from whom all blessings."

Martyr's Prayer

It would have been easy for Anabaptist prisoners to doubt God's leading. Great courage was required to turn away from traditional religion and become members of a persecuted religious minority. Discerning God's will became a necessary, everyday task—and one fraught with danger. With their eyes wide open they needed to listen critically and carefully to preachers and priests and respond with love to their interrogators in the prisons. Yet the Anabaptists persisted in trusting God and treating their enemies with respect. In 1528 eighteen Anabaptists were captured, tortured, and sentenced to the fire at

Salzburg, Austria. Together they wrote the following prayer and left it as a memorial.

Prayer of Eighteen Martyrs at Salzburg

O God of heaven,
  watch over your sheep,
   who are such a little flock,
that we may not depart from you
  or be led astray.
Keep us under your protection...
  and sustain us in your will.
Grant that those who teach false doctrine
  may amend their steps and do your will.
Fill us with your divine power, O God,
  for we have no other Lord in heaven and earth
   but you. Amen.

(VAN BRAGHT, p. 427)

"As the Father has loved me, so I have loved you; abide in my love. If you keep my commandments, you will abide in my love, just as I have kept my Father's commandments and abide in his love. I have said these things to you so that my joy may be in you, and that your joy may be complete."

John 15:9-11

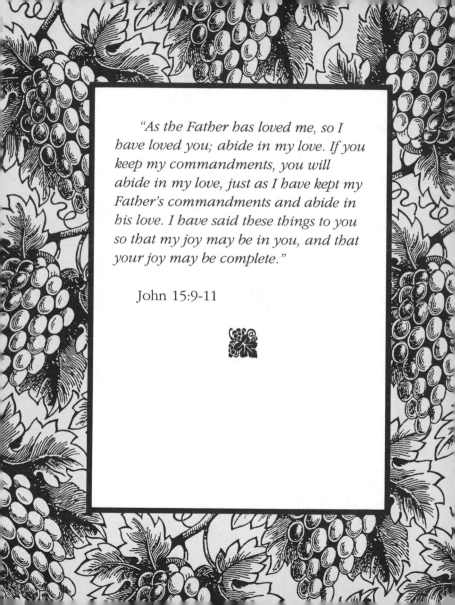

10

Joined in Joy

THE RIGHT combination of successes—in school, work, marriage, finances, relationships—leads to lasting happiness. Or so goes the widely believed myth.

In real life, though, no one lives happily ever after.

"Happy" comes from a word that means "luck" or "chance." The emotion of *happiness* is based on things that *happen*, and life doesn't present any of us with only pleasant events. For all of us, happy feelings, an appropriate response to pleasant circumstances, alternate with feelings of sadness or grief or concern, appropriate responses to unpleasant circumstances. Since happiness hinges on happenings, living happily ever after is just a fairy tale.

But joy is something altogether different. It doesn't depend on circumstances, and so it lasts.

In the hours before his death, Jesus is trying to prepare the eleven for what is about to happen. Judas has already gone out to make final arrangements for Jesus' betrayal. Jesus has already told Peter that he will soon deny knowing him. Jesus has explained that he is about to leave them. And then Jesus says, "I have said these things to you so that my joy may be in you, and that your joy may be complete."

Jesus had endured the most difficult times of his life with joy. Now as he prepares his disciples for the worst hour of their lives, he reveals how they can share in his joy, not just in good times, but even in the most painful of times.

It is here the early Anabaptists followed so closely in Jesus' footsteps. In the midst of their suffering, they spoke often of joy. What was their secret?

It is found in the "these things" Jesus had just told the disciples so his joy might be in them: "Abide in my love. If you keep my commandments, you will abide in my love, just as I have kept my Father's commandments and abide in his love." The secret to continual joy, then, is abiding in Jesus' love.

It sounds pretty ordinary, doesn't it? Sure, we know God loves us, and we're glad. But what does that have to do with being joyful in the midst of suffering?

The answer is, everything. Jesus didn't tell the disciples to go around pretending that bad things didn't happen or that evil was good. That would have been nothing more than self-deceit. If happiness is based on good things happening and we can convince ourselves that everything that happens is good, we can always be happy. But that's not joy. It's a cheap imitation, and it doesn't satisfy.

Rather, Jesus invited the disciples—and us—to look at suffering in light of a greater reality: God's love. Only hours before the most horrific event in human history, the murder of God in the flesh, Jesus' joy remained intact because he knew his Father's love was more powerful than the power of hatred and death that would nail him to the cross. And he knew that no matter how intense the suffering his disciples would face, the power of his love was stronger.

The secret to joy in suffering, then, is not in denying the pain, but in focusing on, abiding in, a greater reality: God's great love and care for us.

Those who abide in God's love—which includes all who keep Jesus' commandments—can be confident not only that God cares when we hurt, not only that God is with us during the suffering, but also that it is God's nature to redeem suffering, to take even what was intended for evil and use it for good (Gen. 50:20). Joy in suffering comes not through blinding ourselves to the reality of evil but in opening our eyes to the even greater reality of God's love for us. When we feel intensely loved in the midst of our suffering, suffering cannot take our joy away.

And how do we experience this love? Of course, Scripture and the Holy Spirit testify of God's love for us. But just as God's love was made incarnate for the disciples in the person of Jesus, God's love becomes incarnate for us in the body of Christ. Knowing that the body of Christ is ready to stand with us in our time of need, out of love, is cause for great joy and a source of great strength.

This is the attitude that so amazed, puzzled, and impressed those who tried, figuratively and literally, to crush the lifeblood out of the early Anabaptists. That joy can continue to amaze, puzzle, and impress today. And it will, so long as we who follow Jesus abide in his love, and so live, in good times and bad, in the fullness of his joy.

Anabaptist Voices

The emphasis on joy among the Anabaptists comes as a surprise. We would not ordinarily expect a persecuted people to be a joyful people, yet that is precisely what they were. Their joy was firmly rooted in their experience of God's love and their trust in God's good purposes. Pilgram Marpeck explained it this way:

> Our highest joy shall be that, in heaven, our names
> are written in the Book of Life (Luke 10:20). To show,
> with unwavering faith and certain hope, love toward
> the neighbour, and thus prove our love of God, is and
> shall be our highest joy. Not the work, but love itself,
> to serve and to be a guardian of the salvation of all
> the elect of God is heavenly joy (MARPECK, p. 437).

Hans Denck looked forward to a future time when the joy of the righteous would be vindicated. When, in the presence of God they would fully understand God's good purposes, it would be like a "rosy splendored dawn" or "rain upon an altogether barren earth." Then, Denck continues, the righteous will say "with great joy in all gentleness and patience, 'Now I know, Lord, that your intention with me in all testing and tribulation is wonderfully good'" (BAUMAN, p. 221).

Guided Prayer Exercise: Prayer of Thanksgiving

Jesus wanted his disciples to be filled with the same joy he had known in following God's will. In the midst of all our experiences, Jesus wants each of us to be full of joy as well.

The prayer of reflection (introduced in session one) can be a discipline for becoming more aware of our true source of joy. If you want to pray a reflective prayer of thanksgiving, follow these steps.

1. Listen to the hymn "Sometimes a light surprises" (Hymnal, 603).

2. Invite the Spirit of God to illuminate your reflections.

3. Look back over the day (or week) and recall moments of joy. What brought a smile or a deep sense of contentment or peace? Where were you aware of God's grace? Give thanks to God for all the gifts you received.

4. Then recall moments of sorrow, pain, or drudgery. What was the source of your grief or unhappiness? Were you also aware of God's presence in the midst of disturbance? What do you want from God in these situations? Express your deepest desires and longings to God. Ask for joy even in the midst of pain.

5. Hold before God those who are suffering within your own congregation. As you become aware of specific people or situations, imagine God's arms surrounding the sufferers, bringing comfort and peace. Pray that God will fill them with joy and a deep sense of God's presence. Give thanks for God's care.

6. Close your prayer by singing or listening to the hymn "Sometimes a light surprises."

Martyr's Prayer

Over and over again the martyrs are described as full of joy on their way to be burned, drowned, or hanged. Such was the case of Maria van Beckum and her sister-in-law Ursula in the city of Delden, Holland, in 1544.

Because of her faith, Maria was driven from her home by her own mother. She fled to her brother John's home, where she was found and arrested by the authorities. Ursula joined her sister-in-law and said, "I will gladly go with you, and we will rejoice together in the Lord."

After much questioning the two women were sentenced to death, and they rejoiced that they were counted worthy to suffer for the name of Christ.

According to the account in Martyrs Mirror, many people who were watching wept as the two women were led to the stake. But the women sang for joy and said, "Weep not on account of what is inflicted upon us. We do not suffer as witches or other criminals, but because we adhere to Christ, and will not be separated from God; hence be converted, and it shall be well with you forever."

At the stake Maria begged the authorities not to shed any more innocent blood. Then she knelt and prayed fervently for those who were to put her to death, arose joyfully, and "went with such great gladness to the stake, that it cannot be told."

Prayer of Maria van Beckum

To you, O Christ,
  I have given myself;
    I know that I shall live with you forever.
Therefore, O God of heaven,
  into your hands do I commend my spirit. Amen.
(VAN BRAGHT, pp. 467-68)

PART 3

Bearing Fruit

"Those who abide in me and I in them bear much fruit, because apart from me you can do nothing."

John 15:5

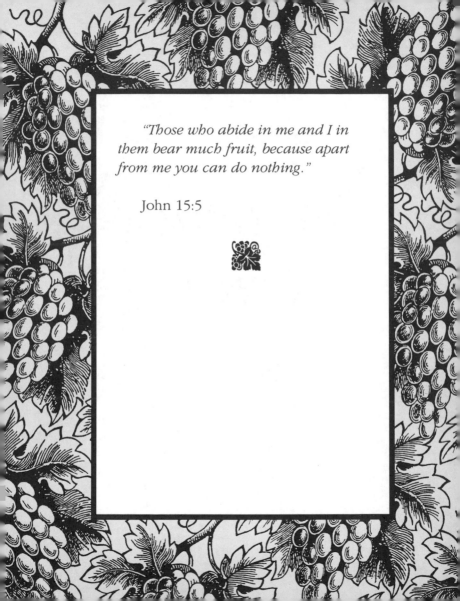

11

Bearing Fruit: The Secret of Productivity

OUR SOCIETY loves results. It showers applause, awards, and wealth on athletes who can hit the most home runs or make the most touchdowns. It admires the executive who can take over a failing business and turn it into a thriving enterprise. It celebrates the successful completion of a spectacular space flight.

Even modern-day Anabaptists, who assign less significance to Heisman trophies, Dun and Bradstreet ratings, and space walks than some others do, tend to be no less result-oriented. While some Christians may be content to enjoy their faith privately, we want to make a difference. We want to help usher in the reign of Christ. We're out to change the world.

For those of us who long to build a better world, who want to make life better for those we touch, Jesus told the parable of the vine and branches. This parable, perhaps more directly than any other part of Jesus' teaching, is about spiritual productivity. It tells us how to bear fruit.

This parable reveals an astonishing secret, a key to productivity that the world will never suspect. Surprisingly, the greatest clue to this secret is not to be found in what the parable says but in what it does not say. Although the whole parable is about how to bear fruit, never does Jesus command his disciples to bear fruit. The parable is full of commands, but none are commands to bear fruit. They are commands to abide.

So the secret is this: Fruit-bearing is not a command, it is a promise. If you want to bear fruit, Jesus is saying, don't focus on bearing fruit; focus on abiding. Fruit will follow.

It makes sense enough for a branch, but could it really be true when it comes to ministry? To touching people's lives? To changing the world? Could Jesus really mean that such results cannot be achieved by seeking results?

We've heard that "the pursuit of happiness" is a futile pursuit. Happiness is not to be had by pursuing it; it is the by-product of giving one's life to something bigger than personal happiness. In much the same way, spiritual fruitfulness does not come from straining to bear fruit; it comes from abiding.

But what does that mean? It's clear enough what it means for a branch to abide in a vine, but what does it mean, in real life, for you and me to abide in Christ? How do we go about it?

Our first clue is found in John 15:9 where Jesus says,

"Abide in my love." The phrase calls up images that go beyond simply knowing we are loved, or even feeling loved. It suggests being surrounded by love, living within love's protection. It may remind us of places where we have felt unconditionally loved and therefore totally safe. To live so surrounded by love is to live in trust because there is nothing to fear.

Jesus is inviting us to live so aware of his enfolding love that even when we cannot see where obedience will lead, we trust and therefore follow. This love-inspired trust is the first dimension of abiding in Christ.

The second clue is found in John 15:10: "If you keep my commandments, you will abide in my love." Trust and obedience feed each other. Trust emboldens us to obey even in the face of risk. Then when we obey, we more fully experience God's trustworthiness. Greater trust leads to more radical obedience which leads to still greater trust.

And what is this obedience to commandments Jesus speaks of? Does it mean following the teachings of Jesus found in the Gospels? Yes, but it means much more. Remember, Jesus was speaking these words not to an anonymous crowd but to eleven intimate friends. His commands to them had included not only public teaching but also one-on-one instruction and guidance.

To apply Jesus' teaching to our lives merely as ethical law is to obey as a servant, but Jesus told the disciples that he no longer regarded them as servants but as friends (v. 15). The obedience of the friend is fuller and more joyful, because the friend is motivated not by outward authority but by inner love and the Spirit's guidance.

"There are two kinds of obedience," Michael Sattler wrote. "The servile looks to the outward and prescribed command of his Lord; the filial is attentive to the inner witness and the Spirit.... The filial is not contrary to the servile, as it might appear, but better and higher. Therefore, let [the one] who is in the servile, seek after a better [obedience] which is the filial, which needs the servile not at all."

Trust and obey. That is how we abide in Christ. And Jesus promises that if we abide, we will bear fruit.

Anabaptist Voices

The leaders of the sixteenth-century Anabaptists were honest people who cared about integrity. They were concerned that those who called themselves Christians would in fact, bear Christ-like fruit. They knew for certain that, on their own, human beings could not produce the fruit that was a mark of being a disciple. But they were also concerned about churches that did not call people to righteous living. How could they resolve this dilemma?

Michael Sattler, who was the chief architect of the Schleitheim Confession in 1527, wrote about a "middle way" that did not fall into the trap of works or the trap of faith without works:

Blessed be [the one] who remains on the middle path, who turns aside neither to the work-righteous (who

promised blessedness or the forgiveness of sins
through works done without faith), preaching works
in such a way that they think no more of faith, so that
all their works are like wild plums, ceremonies without faith. Nor to the side of the scribes, who although
they have forsaken works, then turn aside to the right
and teach in the name of "gospel" a faith without
works and take the poor obedient Christ (who had no
place to lay his head, who speaks without complaint
or self-defense) as their satisfaction, but will not hear
what he says, "Come, follow me" (HAAS, p. 69).

In a carefully written theological treatise, Balthasar
Hubmaier described the human and divine partnership
that produces the true fruit of discipleship.

Since however a [person] knows and confesses that
by nature he is a bad and poisonous tree and that in
himself he cannot produce any good fruit, this commitment, consent and open witness [of baptism] does
not take place in human power or ability ... but in the
name of God ... that is, in the grace and power of
God. Therefore [the person] has also become willing
from now on openly to confess faith in the name of
Jesus Christ before everyone and has committed himself and decided to live from now on according to the
word and commandment of Christ, not from human
ability ... but in the power of God. Now [the person]
breaks out in word and deed, announces and magni-

fies the name and praise of Christ in order that others through us may become holy and blessed ... that the kingdom of Christ may be increased (KLAASSEN, p. 166).

Guided Prayer Exercise: Prayer of Abiding

Even in our life of prayer we may get caught trying to be a "success." If we pray often enough and hard enough and in the right ways, surely our lives will produce the fruit of righteousness.

Instead of trying harder, Jesus told his disciples to "abide," to "be" with him. But in a production-minded culture, we can hardly imagine what it means to "be" with Christ. Centering prayer (introduced in chapter 4) is one way Christians through the centuries have practiced "being" with Christ.

If you want to practice centering prayer as a way of abiding in Christ, follow these steps.

1. Listen to the hymn "Prince of peace, control my will" (Hymnal, 534).

2. Spend a few moments becoming quiet. Light a candle as a symbol of Christ, the Light. Ask God to fill you with a sense of Christ's presence.

3. Remain quietly aware of Christ, not doing anything or trying to form words to speak. Just "be" in the presence of Christ. If you find your mind wandering or your body becoming fidgety, focus your attention again on the candle, the symbol of Christ's presence.

4. When you find yourself quietly at peace, open your heart to the Spirit's voice. Is there anything God wants to say to you? If you don't sense God is speaking to you, continue resting in God's presence. If you hear the voice of God, respond with an open heart.

5. Give God thanks for being with you. Ask for the gift of a deeper sense of Christ's presence in your life.

6. Sing or listen to the hymn "Prince of peace, control my will."

Martyr's Prayer

In their long and lonely days in prison, the Anabaptists had many hours to "be" with Christ. They experienced his love and companionship and, more and more, became united with God's purposes in the world. The fruit of this relationship was expressed in the courage with which they faced death, the love they showed to their captors, and the deep hope they shared for the unity and health of the church.

Two martyrs, Vilgard and Caspar of Schoeneck, were beheaded for their faith at Ries in the Tyrol district of Austria about the year 1528. They died as faithful witnesses of Jesus Christ and left a letter of encouragement for their sisters and brothers in the church. They wrote, "Praise God with shouting, young and old, great and small; you who have believed His Word, love God as His dear children, and walk before Him with pure hearts, and you shall never be forsaken, but He will ... preserve you" (VAN BRAGHT, p. 429).

Prayer of Vilgard and Caspar of Schoeneck

O God,
  you are rich in grace.
Keep us, your children,
  that we may hold to you
    so those who have come to you
      will not be confounded.
Lead us diligently with your right hand
  into the promised land,
    your eternal heavenly kingdom.
Honor be unto you, O God,
  in your high throne.
You have given us Christ, your Son,
  and imparted divine grace to us.
We now confess you with heart and mouth.
Praised be your holy name. Amen.

                    (VAN BRAGHT, p. 429)

"As you have sent me into the world, so I have sent them into the world."

John 17:18

12

Bearing the Fruit of Loving Service

HAVE YOU EVER watched someone grow, at least partly because of your help? It's a rewarding feeling, isn't it? It is our privilege, as branches in the vine, to be channels of God's transforming love.

Yet the desire to make a difference can sometimes become a trap. When Art moved to the inner city to minister among the poor, he was driven by a passion to make life better for hurting people. It's an admirable motive, but, as Art discovered, it's not enough. Here in his own words is Art's story. Names and certain details have been changed to protect privacy.

"Which should I do—become a bag lady or commit myself to the mental hospital?" She was sitting on my front step when she asked, her gray-white hair pulled up into a topknot, her face drawn tight.

Inwardly I shouted protest, but outwardly, with a

123

calm I didn't feel, I asked, "What do you think?"

A Christian for about two years, Florence was eager to grow spiritually, confident of God's power to heal her mental illness, and highly motivated to reach her goal of living independently. But in spite of her faith and the support of a caring church fellowship, Florence was not doing well.

One day Florence told me her neighbor had been trying to scare her into moving by transmitting frightening thoughts into her mind. As we talked, I didn't tell her what I thought was real or imagined. I just asked questions to help her sort it out for herself. She seemed to leave more in touch with reality, and I felt encouraged.

But her good times never lasted long. In time Florence grew depressed, stopped eating regularly, and started neglecting her medication, so I helped arrange for her to live temporarily in a group home. There she received regular psychological counseling, job counseling, and training in basic living skills.

After three months she returned to our neighborhood and started a job in a sheltered workplace. Her first week back in church with us Florence seemed like a new woman. We celebrated with her!

But before long she again found the stresses of daily life overwhelming. She quit her job, withdrew into her home, and stopped coming to church. One day she asked me, "Do you think there are some people God never intended to take care of themselves?" I could tell Florence was giving up on her dream.

That afternoon when Florence sat on my steps, unemployed, unemployable, and frustrated in her attempts to collect disability, eviction was imminent. Even if someone else paid her back rent, she knew that would only postpone the inevitable.

The streets? Or a mental hospital? That day I listened, really listened, and was able to let go of my illusion that Florence could or should see her situation as I saw it or choose what I would choose. I began to see Florence's situation, to a degree at least, through her eyes. I never did offer Florence any advice that day, but by the time she headed home, she no longer seemed lost, but confident and decisive. A few weeks later she admitted herself to the state mental hospital.

Florence had wanted desperately to hold a job and live in her own home. I had worked hard to help her reach that goal. And I had failed. The months at the group home, the counseling, the financial help, the sheltered workplace, scores of hours of being with and doing for Florence—all wasted.

Wasted? No, because for a couple of years, at least, Florence had known she was loved. She had belonged.

Even more important, perhaps, was what Florence had taught me. I had thought I accepted Florence. I had cared about her, invested time and energy in her. I had been patient and firm—sometimes comforting, other times confrontive.

Maybe that was love, but it was not unconditional. For along with all my hours of giving, I had expecta-

tions. I expected change, growth, results. It was not until that day on our steps as I listened to Florence with new ears that I truly accepted her, not for who she might become but for who she was.

It was through Florence that I first heard God say, "I don't call you to love people only when your love brings results; I call you to love people because each person needs and deserves love simply by virtue of being a person.

We, like Jesus, are sent into the world to live out God's love. Sometimes God's love will have the transforming effect we hope for. Other times, as with Florence, no amount of loving service will make our dreams come true. And sometimes people will reject God's love.

Yet in sending us into the world, Jesus doesn't tell us to change people's lives. He only asks that we bear the fruit of loving as he loved. Even when results seem unlikely.

Anabaptist Voices

Not to serve was not an option for the Anabaptists. As automatic as breathing, serving others—both within the church and beyond—was an indisputable sign of the indwelling Spirit. Jesus came to serve. Those who followed him would also become servants.

From her prison cell in Rotterdam, Holland, in 1573, Maeyken van Deventer wrote a last testament to her children, Albert, Johan, Egbert, and Truyken. In her letter she told them she could not leave them silver or gold or any of this world's treasures. What she could give them was instruction that would lead them to the eternal riches of salvation. After calling them to love and follow Christ, she described in detail what it would mean to be a follower of Christ.

> My children, love your neighbor heartily, and this with a liberal heart. Let the light of the Gospel shine in you.... Deal your bread to the hungry, clothe the naked, and do not suffer anything to remain with you double, since there are enough that lack (Isaiah 58:7). And whatsoever the Lord grants you, that possess with thankfulness, not only for yourselves, but also for your neighbor, and seek not your own profit, but that of your neighbor. In short, my children, let your life be conformed to the Gospel of Christ (VAN BRAGHT, p. 979).

In a discussion of baptism, Balthasar Hubmaier wrote about the importance of serving by sharing possessions: "Each [person] should have regard for his neighbor, so that the hungry might be fed, the thirsty refreshed, the naked clothed. For we are not lords of our own property, but stewards and dispensers" (KLAASSEN, p. 233).

Along the same lines, Menno Simons described the true children of God as citizens of a heavenly realm who "use the lower creations such as eating, drinking, clothing, and shelter, with thanksgiving and to the necessary support of their own lives, and to the free service of their neighbor, according to the Word of the Lord" (KLAASSEN, pp. 109-110).

Guided Prayer Exercise: Prayer of Preparation for Service

Biblical religion has always dealt harshly with those who engage in religious acts but do not act with love and mercy in the world. In the letter of James, the question is raised: "If a brother or sister is naked and lacks daily food, and one of you says to them, 'Go in peace; keep warm and eat your fill,' and yet you do not supply their bodily needs, what is the good of that?" (James 2:15-16).

One might also ask: What is the good of praying when people need food or clothing or medicine? Wouldn't we be better off going out to serve than spending time in prayer?

Such a question is typical of North Americans. Tuned in to efficiency and productivity and results, we find it easier to get on with the action than to become lovers of the people we are sent to serve. Unfortunately, our serving is sometimes tainted with our own self-interests, our need to impress others, or our desire to control people. Jesus asks us to serve as he served—with a heart overflowing with love, making no demands, simply offering the free gifts of grace.

The only way to serve as Jesus served is to stay in daily contact with Jesus, remaining open to the Spirit's cleansing and guidance. If you want to pray a prayer of preparation for service, follow these steps:

1. Listen to the hymn "Forth in thy name" (Hymnal, 415).

2. Quiet your heart and mind, asking for the grace of a humble heart.

3. Recall the ways you have given yourself in service to others in the past. Did you serve out of a sense of duty or as a free response to God's love and grace? What were your expectations in serving? Did you want to make a difference? What was your attitude toward the people you served? If the Spirit brings unwholesome attitudes or actions to your awareness, confess them to God. Ask for forgiveness and receive cleansing.

4. Recall times when you may have passed up an opportunity to serve. You were too busy or did not care about someone in need. Perhaps you promised to help and then did not follow through. Again, if the Spirit makes you aware of failings, confess them to God. Ask for forgiveness and receive cleansing.

5. Wait in silence for a few moments, resting in the comfort of God's love and care. Then invite the Spirit to show you where you are being called to serve. How can you freely share the love of Christ—in your neighborhood, at your job, or in a place of need? Can you give away some of your possessions? Write a letter of encouragement? Babysit for someone's children? Spend time at a shelter for the homeless? Ask for strength and courage to follow the Spirit's leading.

6. Give thanks for the example of Jesus who shows us how to serve in love.

7. Close your prayer by singing or listening to the hymn "Forth in thy name."

Martyr's Prayer

Hans Langmantel, a wealthy German citizen of noble descent, was converted in 1529 along with his manservant and maidservant. After the three of them were baptized, they were imprisoned and endured much torture. When they refused to give up their faith, Hans and his manservant were beheaded with the sword, and the maidservant was drowned. While they were still in prison, they wrote a prayer and letter of encouragement to their sisters and brothers.

Prayer of Hans Langmantel and his manservant and maidservant

O God,
  preserve us in your keeping,
    that we may not faint and abandon your Word.
  Let us enjoy the faithfulness which you have shown
    through your Son Jesus Christ.
  Kindle in us the fire of your divine love;
    lead us to practice love as your dear children.
  Let the light of your divine glory illuminate us,
    that we may walk in it.

O God,
  we ask you for one thing more:
    send us your Holy Spirit,
    endue us with power,

renew our hearts,
and make us strong in you
that we may obey you
and praise your name. Amen.

(VAN BRAGHT, p. 430)

Peace I leave with you; my peace I give to you. I do not give to you as the world gives. Do not let your hearts be troubled, and do not let them be afraid.

John 14:27

13

Bearing the Fruit of Peacemaking

WHO WOULDN'T LIKE to wake up one morning and hear a newscaster say, "Today the world is at peace!" What a relief it would be to hear that every conflict between nations and individuals had been resolved.

Instead of stories of violence, the news media would be telling stories of peace. Children would be free to play games in parks and streets; teenagers could ride city buses in safety; elderly women and men would walk without fear in the daytime or nighttime. Instead of buying guns to defend themselves, people would bring all their weapons to be melted down into statues for peace. Flowers and grass would grow again in vacant alleys and empty city lots where people had been afraid to loiter.

In the political capitals of the world, heads of government would call together the brightest, most creative thinkers to brainstorm ways to transform munitions manufacturing plants into production centers for peace industries. All the armies of the world would be dismantled and sent home. Everyone—from the youngest children to the oldest grandparents—would be trained to resolve conflicts with peaceful, nonviolent strategies.

An impossible dream? Not at all.

Jesus promised his disciples the gift of peace. In a world where naked power and violence often gain the upper hand, Jesus refused to be trapped by false assumptions that separate and divide people. He offered an alternative way of feeling, thinking, and living—a gift more valuable than anything the world could offer.

Peace was a recurring theme in Jesus' conversation, especially after the resurrection. When Jesus joined his fearful followers on the evening of the day he was raised from the dead, his first words were, "Peace be with you." Once the disciples recognized him and began rejoicing, he repeated his greeting: "Peace be with you" (John 20:19-21).

A week later when the disciples had gathered again, Jesus came and stood among them. Again he repeated his reassuring greeting: "Peace be with you" (John 20:26).

Did they recall Jesus' words of comfort and promise from the days just before he died? Within their locked room, did they remember the promise that they would never need to be afraid again?

One of the sad and exasperating realities of life at the end of the twentieth century is that so few people remember or are willing to risk trusting the promise Jesus made. Instead of receiving Jesus' gift of peace, we persist in fortifying ourselves against other people and nations. We lock our doors. We defend our towns and cities. We strangle our economies with taxes for military spending.What is the root of the problem? Very simply, Jesus says that the problem is fear. When people do not rest in God's promises, they become afraid. And fear begets violence.

Henri Nouwen observes, "Most of us people of the twentieth century live in the house of fear most of the time. It has become an obvious dwelling place, an acceptable basis on which to make our decisions and plan our lives" (NOUWEN, p. 15). When fear becomes so commonplace, it is no wonder that people can hardly hear Jesus' words or risk trusting Jesus' promise of peace.

What Jesus offers is an alternative to fear, an intimate relationship with God in which we are like branches securely attached to a life-giving Vine. Within the safety of such a relationship we open ourselves to God's love which cleanses and transforms our fear-filled hearts. The urge to protect and fortify is replaced with a desire to love and make peace.

But such a transformation cannot be maintained without the close companionship of other Christians. Because the world around us is so contaminated with fear and violence, we will inevitably succumb to its destructive influence if we are not part of a circle of people who are also committed to love and peace. Within the intimacy of a community of Christ's followers, we find courage to face our fears and confess our sins. We learn to trust, to forgive, and to reach out with open hands and hearts to everyone God has created.

The gift of peace, as wonderful as it is, is not just for the benefit of individual Christians or communities of Christians. It is meant to be the foundation for a way of living in the world. As a trademark of Jesus' followers, it characterizes all their attitudes and actions, private as well as public. Even enemies are to be loved without fear.

An amazing event that reveals this radical commitment to peace and love of enemies took place in 1569 in Asperen, Holland. Dirk Willems, a faithful Anabaptist, was being hotly pursued by a thief-catcher who intended to imprison him for his faith. When Dirk ran across a frozen river in an attempt to elude his captor, the thief-catcher followed and fell through the ice. Dirk heard his cries and immediately came back to pull him out of the river. The thief-catcher was grateful that his life had been saved and wanted to release Dirk. The local authorities had no mercy, however, and ordered Dirk to be imprisoned. He was burned at the stake on May 16, 1569.

When Christians trust God in life as well as death, they are set free to become peacemakers. With nothing to lose and everything to gain, they are truly the children of God.

Anabaptist Voices

One of the remarkable characteristics of early Anabaptists was their commitment to peacemaking despite its cost. Even though they were misunderstood by family members, persecuted by civil and religious authorities, and martyred at the stake, they persisted in following

Christ's way of love in the world.

Their commitment to peacemaking was based squarely on their commitment to Christ. Menno Simons, who often wrote about peace, stated emphatically:

> The Prince of peace is Christ Jesus; His kingdom is the kingdom of peace, which is His church. His messengers are the messengers of peace; His Word is the word of peace; His body is the body of peace; His children are the seed of peace; His inheritance and reward are the inheritance and reward of peace. In short, with this King, and in His kingdom and reign, it is nothing but peace. Everything that is seen, heard, and done is peace (WENGER, p. 554).

Conrad Grebel, who was an early leader in Zurich, Switzerland, and one of the first Anabaptists to be rebaptized, wrote of one implication of their commitment to peacemaking:

> The gospel and its adherents are not to be protected by the sword, nor are they thus to protect themselves.... All killing has ceased with them (KLAASSEN, p. 267).

The reason Christians do not kill, according to the Anabaptists, is that their primary citizenship is in heaven, not in this world. Michael Sattler wrote, "The weapons of the Christians are spiritual, against the fortification of the devil. The worldly are armed with steel and iron, but Christians are armed with the armor of God, with truth, righteousness, peace, faith, salvation, and with the Word of God" (KLAASSEN, p. 269).

Beyond refusing to participate in physical violence, Anabaptists also abhorred mental or emotional violence. Hans Denck wrote, "No Christian, who wishes to boast in his Lord may use power to coerce and rule" (KLAASSEN, p. 270).

These followers of Christ even refused to take revenge on those who had wronged them. Menno Simons wrote:

> True Christians do not know vengeance, no matter how they are mistreated. In patience they possess their souls.... And they do not break their peace, even if they should be tempted by bondage, torture, poverty, and besides, by the sword and fire. They do not cry, Vengeance, vengeance, as does the world; but with Christ they supplicate and pray: Father, forgive them; for they know not what they do.
>
> According to the declaration of the prophets they have beaten their swords into plowshares and their spears into pruning hooks. They shall sit every man under his vine and under his fig-tree, Christ; neither shall they learn war anymore (WENGER, p. 555).

As branches abiding in the vine, the Anabaptists trusted Christ for their very life. And if their commitment to the way of love cost them their earthly lives, they rejoiced in suffering for the sake of Christ. With all their hearts, they believed that God's peaceful purposes would triumph in the end.

Guided Prayer Exercise: Prayer for Peace

One way to join with God's work of making peace in the world is to pray with love for our enemies and for those who suffer. If you want to participate in prayer as peacemaking, follow these suggested steps.

1. Listen to the hymn "O day of peace" (Hymnal, 408).

2. Wait in silence until your spirit is at rest. Reflect on the gift of peace you have received from Christ. Give thanks for "the peace of God, which surpasses all understanding" (Philippians 4:7).

3. Ask God to fill your heart with a spirit of compassion. Then imagine the members of your family—grandparents, parents, sisters or brothers, children, grandchildren. As each one passes by in your imagination, pray a blessing of peace upon them. If you become aware of fear or anger or unresolved conflicts, place your burden in God's hands. Let the love of Christ flow through you to your family.

4. Then let your imagination extend to your town, your region, or your country. Ask the Spirit to show you where the gift of peace is needed. As you become aware of specific situations or people, pray a blessing of peace upon them. Imagine the love of Christ transforming fearful or violent people into people of peace.

5. Open your heart still further to the whole world. Imagine a globe turning before your mind's eye. As nations and continents pass before you, wait for the Spirit to bring to your attention certain places or situations of violence, poverty, or oppression. Let your heart be touched with the pain of those who suffer. Pray for the love of Christ to be shared in each place. Ask God to bless the world with peace.

6. If you become aware of enemies during this prayer, pray for forgiveness. Ask to see your enemies as God sees them. Open your heart to love all whom God loves.

7. As you end your prayer, listen for any direction from the Spirit about ways you can make peace in your world. Give thanks for all who work for peace and ask God to keep them strong and full of hope and love.

8. Close by singing or listening to the hymn "O day of peace."

Martyr's Prayer

George Blaurock, a priest who became an Anabaptist preacher, was a member of the first group of Anabaptists in Zurich. During four years of short but fruitful ministry, he is reported to have baptized over one thousand people in northern Switzerland and the Tyrol.

Among the group of early believers, Felix Manz was the first to be martyred. He died by drowning in the Limmat River on January 5, 1527. On the same day George Blaurock was stripped to the waist and whipped out of town. In 1529 Blaurock and several companions were apprehended, imprisoned, condemned for their faith, and burned alive.

With his fellow minister Hans van der Reve, Blaurock wrote the following prayer from prison to console and strengthen other believers.

Prayer of George Blaurock and Hans van der Reve

Lord God,
I will praise you now and until my end
because you have given me faith,
by which I have learned to know you.
When I felt the heavy load of sin in me,
you came to me with the Word of your divine grace.
For this I will now magnify and praise your glorious
name forever.
Strengthen my faith, O Lord.
Do not forget me,
but be with me always.
Protect and teach me with your Holy Spirit
that in all my sufferings I may receive your consolation.

Dear Lord,
help me to bear the cross to the destined place,
and turn yourself to me with all grace,
that I may commend my spirit into your hands.
I sincerely pray for all my enemies, O Lord,

however many there may be.
Do not lay their sins to their charge.
Lord, I entreat this according to your will.
May God finish his holy work
  and give strength to the end. Amen.

(VAN BRAGHT, pp. 431-32)

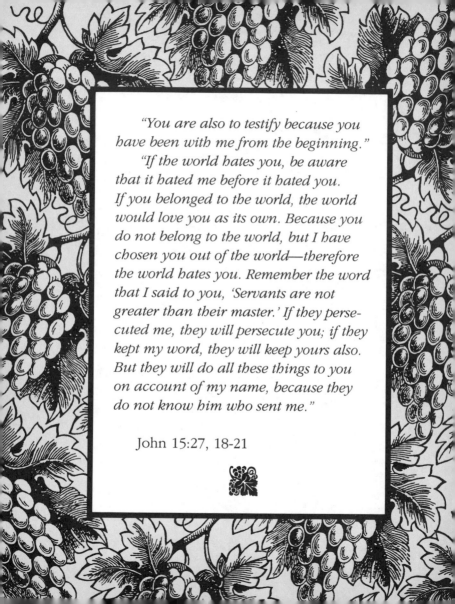

"You are also to testify because you have been with me from the beginning."

"If the world hates you, be aware that it hated me before it hated you. If you belonged to the world, the world would love you as its own. Because you do not belong to the world, but I have chosen you out of the world—therefore the world hates you. Remember the word that I said to you, 'Servants are not greater than their master.' If they persecuted me, they will persecute you; if they kept my word, they will keep yours also. But they will do all these things to you on account of my name, because they do not know him who sent me."

John 15:27, 18-21

14

Bearing the Fruit of Witness

IF TOMORROW'S MAIL brought you an invitation to meet with the president or prime minister of your country, how would you respond? Would you quietly file the letter away and go on to opening your junk mail? Or would you tell someone?

And a month later, when you returned from your meeting with a head of state, would you calmly unpack your suitcase and go on with your routine as though nothing out of the ordinary had happened? Or would you fill your family and friends in on the highlights of your visit?

When we have experiences that we consider especially significant, we feel compelled to tell others about them. In most cases, it never crosses our minds not to talk about them.

That must have been how it was for the eleven disciples when it came to talking about Jesus. Jesus was their reason for living. I can't imagine talking to any of them for long without finding that out. It's not that they'd go out of their way to witness. Rather, Jesus was so central to their lives that concealing that fact would have taken conscious effort.

How different that is from my early understanding of witnessing. I thought of witnessing simply as trying to persuade non-Christians to become Christians. It was many years before I realized that my definition left out the most critical element. A witness is, first of all, someone who has witnessed something. Because of what the person has witnessed, he or she is qualified to witness or testify about it in a court of law or elsewhere. The prerequisite to witnessing, therefore, is personal experience. Jesus clearly had this in mind when he told the eleven, "You also are to testify because you have been with me from the beginning."

Two of those eleven, when later reprimanded by the Sanhedrin for speaking about Jesus, would answer simply, "We cannot keep from speaking about what we have seen and heard" (Acts 4:20). That was not impudence. That was simply reality for two men whose lives had been powerfully shaped by their relationship with Jesus.

What we give witness to above all else, then, is what God has done and is doing in our lives. To try to persuade others to become Christians when Jesus is not the life-giving center of our own lives may be clever marketing, but it is not witnessing. Bearing witness always begins with personal experience—"what we have seen and heard."

But it doesn't end there. *Martyreo*, the verb translated "*witness*" or "*testify*" in the New Testament, originally referred to giving personal testimony to events or facts. It grew also to mean confessing personal faith based on those events and facts. Finally, it came to mean being a faithful witness even to the point of death, and the Greek word for witness became our word "martyr."

Jesus warned that because the world hated him, it would also hate those who follow him. While those whose lives are defined by their relationship with Jesus will feel compelled to live out and talk about "what they have seen and heard," that does not mean it will be safe.

The early Anabaptists were witnesses who felt compelled to speak. Like the eleven, they could not keep quiet. They testified in homes, on the streets, before princes, on the scaffold, and as flames ascended around them. Still in many parts of the world today, to be a faithful witness is to offer oneself for martyrdom.

Jesus promised his disciples that if they abided in him they would bear fruit and be filled with his joy, but he also promised they would be persecuted. The same promises apply to us. There is nothing more rewarding than to grow in intimacy with God and to know God's work is being done through us. But being a faithful witness involves more—not only the risk but also the certainty of rejection. Jesus didn't say this to scare us, but to prepare us, so we would be ready to endure persecution with joy like the early Anabaptists and the apostles who "rejoiced that they were considered worthy to suffer dishonor for the sake of the name" (Acts 5:41).

May we too so appreciate the activity of God which we witness in our lives and in our world that we cannot help but speak about "what we have seen and heard," no matter the cost.

Anabaptist Voices

To become an Anabaptist in the sixteenth century was risky business. Imprisonment, torture, and death were likely consequences for those whose commitment to Christ caused them to defy the church and the state. The methods of execution were especially cruel, including burning at the stake, being buried alive, or being tied up in a bag and thrown into a river to drown. Many were tortured in attempts to force them to deny their faith. Methods included being stretched on a rack until their bones cracked or having their tongues or limbs pierced with screws or pinched in vises (SMITH, pp. 105-106).

Yet very few of these devoted Christians recanted or implicated their fellow believers. Interestingly, approximately thirty percent of the Anabaptist martyrs were women, compared to six percent for other groups (SMITH, p. 105).

Whether in courtrooms, in prison, or on their way to be executed, the martyrs consistently witnessed to their faith in Jesus Christ and called others to follow him. One such martyr was Maria of Monjou, Belgium, who was imprisoned for over a year. Her account in *Martyrs Mirror* says, "And though she had to suffer much, yet she bore it with joy. Her constant admonition to all the pious was, that they should walk in love, and hold fast the covenant of Jesus Christ."

On the way to her execution, Maria sang with a joyful heart and said, "I have been the bride of a man; but today I hope to be the bride of Christ, and to inherit His kingdom with Him." But her torture had not yet ended. As they came near the water, her captors argued with her for over two hours in an attempt to persuade her to forsake her faith. She steadfastly refused and said, "I adhere to my God; proceed with what you have come here for." Then she undressed, willingly surrendered herself and prayed, "O heavenly Father, into Thy hands I commend my spirit," and died by drowning—sealing her confession with her own life (VAN BRAGHT, pp. 525-526).

Even though many of the Anabaptists escaped death, they lived with the constant threat of imprisonment. It would have been easy for them to keep quiet and practice a secret faith. Menno Simons wrote about what motivated him to continue witnessing for his faith.

> I have sometimes with Jeremiah thought not to teach
> any more in the name of the Lord, because so many
> seek my life. Yet, I can no longer hold my tongue, for
> I am with the prophet very much troubled at heart;
> my heart trembles in me; all my joints shake and
> quake when I consider that the whole world, lords,
> princes, learned and unlearned people, men and
> women, bond and free are so estranged from Christ
> Jesus and from evangelical truth and from life eternal
> (WENGER, p. 298).

Therefore, we preach, as much as is possible, both by day and by night, in houses and in fields, in forests and wastes, hither and yon, at home or abroad, in prisons and in dungeons, in water and in fire, on the scaffold and on the wheel, before lords and princes, through mouth and pen, with possessions and blood, with life and death. We have done this these many years, and we are not ashamed of the Gospel of the glory of Christ (WENGER, p. 633).

Guided Prayer Exercise: Praying the "Jesus Prayer"

One of the ways Christians through the centuries have carried with them a sense of the presence of Christ and, out of that union, witnessed to others was by praying what is called the "Jesus Prayer."

If you want to pray the Jesus Prayer, follow these suggestions:

1. Find a quiet place to listen to the hymn "How buoyant and bold the stride" (Hymnal, 394).

2. Relax your mind and body by quietly breathing in and out. Then, when your heart is still, repeat the prayer "Lord Jesus Christ, have mercy on me" each time you breathe. Continue for several minutes.

3. Then think back in your life to the people who shared the good news of Jesus Christ with you. Have you ever thanked them for this gift? Give thanks to God for the gift of salvation you have received and for the faithful testi-

mony of Jesus' followers.

4. Now think of the people who daily walk in and out of your life—family, neighbors, friends, coworkers, mail carriers, sales clerks, and others. Pray the Jesus Prayer for each of them: "Lord Jesus Christ, have mercy." Ask God to show you a way to proclaim your faith to them. Pray that the Spirit of God will blow in their hearts like the wind. (You can also pray this prayer as you meet people. For example, as you wait behind a car at a stoplight, pray the Jesus Prayer on behalf of the person in the next car. Or pray the Jesus Prayer for the server who brings you your food in a restaurant.)

5. Think of people who are giving their lives in active witness for Christ—youth workers, missionaries, pastors, teachers, and others. Pray the Jesus Prayer in their behalf. Pray that God will keep them faithful and make their witness fruitful.

6. Pray for the church around the world as God's people witness to their faith in many different countries and settings. Think especially of the people of God who are suffering or being persecuted for their faith. Pray the Jesus Prayer on behalf of all who follow Christ through pain or persecution.

7. Conclude your prayer by again praying the Jesus Prayer with each breath. Then sing or listen to the hymn "How buoyant and bold the stride."

Martyr's Prayer

Jacob de Roore, known commonly as Jacob the Chandler, a minister in the church, did not allow his imprisonment in Bruges, Flanders, in 1569 to keep him from witnessing about his newfound faith. From prison he wrote many letters to his family and to the church. On April 18, 1569, he wrote:

> My dear brethren and sisters, if we do not abide in Him, it is all labor lost, and we cannot be partakers of His abundant riches.... If we abide not in Him ... we are like a branch that does not abide in the vine, and forthwith withers.... Let your loins be girded about, and your lights burning (VAN BRAGHT, p. 800).

Such steadfastness had its price. To his wife and children Jacob wrote of his great sorrow in their separation. "I pray you, my dear wife," he wrote, "that you ... do not grieve too much on account of this my trial.... For I had thought to come and take leave, but the Lord did not permit me—He knows why it is. Still I am grieving much on your account, for I leave you in great distress. But I hope that the Lord, who has taken me from you, will help you and provide for you, according to His promise, since He feeds the ravens and little animals, because they are His creatures; how much more then shall He provide for his elect, who cry day and night unto him? ... O my dear and beloved wife, it would greatly rejoice me if I could hear that you were of good cheer; for every time that I have written your or the children's names, I could not refrain from weeping" (VAN BRAGHT, pp. 798-99).

This prayer is adapted from writings attributed to Jacob de Roore.

Prayer of Jacob the Chandler

God, our heavenly Father,
   through Jesus Christ, your Son,
  you have given us the Holy Ghost
   that we should be led by Him,
   and guided into all truth,
  in order to be a light in this world.
We praise you for your grace
  and pray that we will remain faithful
   to the end of our life. Amen.

(VAN BRAGHT, p. 800)

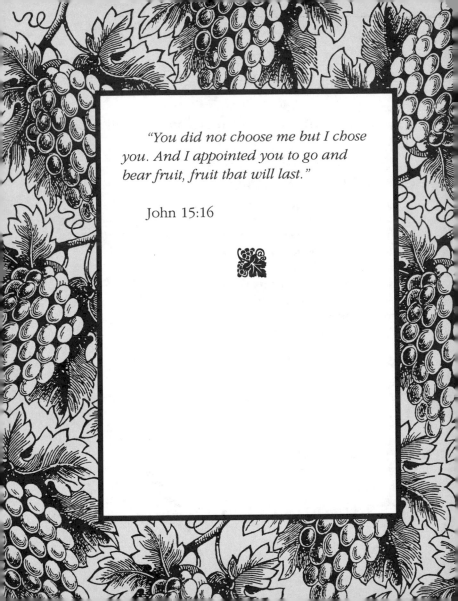

"You did not choose me but I chose you. And I appointed you to go and bear fruit, fruit that will last."

John 15:16

15

Bearing Fruit
That Lasts

SOME FRUIT won't keep. It has to be used at once. Other fruit, though, can be kept all year. And so it is with the fruit of the Christian life. Some do work that looks impressive, but has no lasting effect, while the work of others yields results for generations or eternity.

Paul chooses a different metaphor to contrast the fruit that lasts and the fruit that does not. He describes how each of us builds on the foundation of Jesus Christ using any of various materials—gold, silver, precious stones, wood, hay, or straw. Which of these materials the builder uses may not become visible until the day of the Lord when it will be tested by fire. Some work will survive the test while other work will be burned, even though the builder will be saved (1 Corinthians 3:12-15).

What makes the difference? How can we insure that the fruit we bear stands the test of time?

The answer, of course, is found in what Jesus means by

abiding in the vine. It is true that we cannot bear fruit unless we abide in Jesus, but, unfortunately, we can in our own strength produce results that resemble spiritual fruit—the results that Paul calls hay and straw. It is even possible to start right—with the right foundation—then go astray.

How many of us have heard God's voice, set out to obey, only at some point to take over personally what God set in motion? Remember Abraham? When God promised that he would become the father of many nations, he believed. Yet when God's timing didn't match his expectations, he became impatient and took matters into his own hands, fathering Ishmael. But Ishmael was not the son of promise. In time, Abraham resumed his "abiding" and the miracle son Isaac was born.

God's work cannot be done in human timing or in human wisdom. God's work must be done in God's time, in God's ways, in God's power. And for that to happen through us we must abide—trust and obey. When Abraham acted out of trust and obedience, God's purposes could be fulfilled through him. When he tried to "help God out" by hurrying things along, he got in the way.

All believers are like Abraham in that sometimes we do a better job of abiding than at other times. Sometimes, full of trust in God's love and power, we can boldly set out for "the country that God will show us." Other times, when God seems distant and silent, we may take matters into our own hands.

Fruit that lasts is fruit that grows during those times of abiding—trust in God's love and obedience to the Spirit's guidance. Fruit that doesn't last is that which we have tried to grow through our own efforts. It may have even been set on the vine during a time of trust and obedience, but during its growth, we let our attention stray from the connection between the vine and the branch. Somehow the joint was weakened or partially broken, and the fruit did not receive proper nourishment, and so became unhealthy.

The key to producing fruit that lasts, then, is simply to keep our focus, not on the fruit, but on our connection to the vine. If we care for that connection, fruit—healthy fruit, lasting fruit—will follow.

Anabaptist Voices

The fruit many Anabaptists most wanted God to produce in them was courage to remain faithful to the end of their lives. As they remained firmly attached to Jesus, the true vine, they trusted God to fill them with Jesus' own steadfastness. Even through suffering, their desire was to endure whatever trials came with grateful, contented hearts.

From his home in Germany in 1558, Menno Simons wrote to the Christians in Amsterdam during a plague:

Elect brethren and sisters in the Lord, I hear that the fire of pestilence is beginning to rage in your vicinity. Therefore I am constrained by the love which I bear to you... to write you a letter of consolation.

Be strong in the Lord, be of good cheer, be comforted. For your whole life and death is lodged in the hands of the Lord.

We ought not to dread death so. It is but to cease from sin and to enter into a better life. How greatly and gloriously are [the saints] gifted of God who, in grace, delivered from the body of sin, and from the emptiness of all transitory things, are taken up into the holy tabernacles of peace, summoned to the eternal, holy Sabbath.

The old, crooked serpent shall no longer bite them in their heels. No ache nor ill shall touch them more. Their tears are washed away, and their souls are in lasting rest and peace in the Paradise of grace, Abraham's bosom, under the altar of God (HAAS, p. 345-346).

A similar confidence in God's good future was expressed by many martyrs as they awaited death. From her prison cell in Antwerp in 1551, Lijsken Dircks wrote to comfort and encourage her husband, Jerome Segers, who was also in prison:

My dear, beloved husband in the Lord, you have partly passed through the trial, and have remained steadfast, eternal praise and glory to the Lord for His great grace! And I beseech the Lord with tears, to make me also fit, to suffer for His name; ... I commend you to the Lord, and to the word of His grace and glory;

with which He will glorify us, if we adhere to it unto the end (VAN BRAGHT, p. 518).

According to the record, Jerome remained steadfast and was burned at the stake. Lijsken, who was pregnant, first delivered her child and then was "thrust into a bag early in the morning, between three and four o'clock, and murderously thrown into the Scheldt and drowned, before people were up. Nevertheless, there were some that saw it, who testified to her firm and steadfast faith unto death" (VAN BRAGHT, p. 504).

Guided Prayer Exercise: Prayer Anticipating the Future

In many of the prayer exercises in this book, you have been encouraged to look back over your life and become aware of how God has been at work. In this prayer exercise, you will be invited to look ahead to your future and imagine yourself in the presence of Christ.

If you want to pray a prayer anticipating the future, follow the suggested steps.

1. Listen to the hymn "Who now would follow Christ" (Hymnal, 535).

2. Become quiet by breathing deeply and relaxing your mind and body. Invite the Spirit of God to fill you with a sense of peace.

3. Look ahead to the future and imagine yourself at the end of your life. What kind of person will you have

become? What will you have accomplished? How do you feel about what you see? Are you satisfied? Dissatisfied? If you could change anything, what would it be?

4. Then imagine that Jesus joins you in this reflection. Ask Jesus to show you what "fruit" in your life will last. What does Jesus help you see? You may want to write down what you become aware of.

5. Let your imagination extend further to include your church in the future. Ask Jesus to show you what "fruit" in the life of your congregation will endure. What does Jesus help you see? Again you may want to write down your reflections.

6. Invite the Spirit of God to reveal to you what needs to be changed or transformed in your life or in your congregation for lasting fruit to be produced. Ask for grace to begin making those changes. Give thanks to God who makes all things new.

7. Think about whom you might share your reflections with. Your pastor? Sunday school class? Small group? A trusted friend?

8. Close your prayer by singing or listening to "Who now would follow Christ."

Martyr's Prayer

Anna of Freiburg, Germany, was a zealous new convert who was baptized and "sought to arise with Christ; and walk in newness of life" (VAN BRAGHT, p. 434). But like many other Anabaptists, she was apprehended by the authorities, tortured, and sentenced to death in 1529. Not content to kill her once, her captors dealt her a double punishment. Anna was drowned in water and afterward burned with fire.

Prayer of Anna of Freiburg

Dear eternal, heavenly Father,
I call upon you from the depths of my heart;
do not let me turn from you,
but keep me in your truth unto my end.
Instruct and teach me,
your poor, unworthy child,
that I may press even unto death,
through all sorrows, sufferings, anguish and pain.
Let me persevere, O God,
that I may not be separated from your love.

Comfort me by your holy word,
in which I firmly trust.
I commend myself to you and your church.

Be my Protector today,
for your holy name's sake,
through Jesus Christ. Amen.

(VAN BRAGHT, pp. 434-435)

Biographies of Selected Sixteenth-Century Anabaptists

Maria and Ursula van Beckum

Because she chose to remain steadfast to her Anabaptist beliefs, Maria van Beckum lost her family, home, and ultimately, her life. In 1544 her mother forced her to leave her home and she sought refuge with her brother. Later, she was arrested at her brother's home. Upon seeing the large crowd that had come to apprehend her, Maria begged her sister-in-law, Ursula, to go with her.

Together, the two young women were taken to Deventer in Holland and then to Delden, where they were questioned by friars and commissary officials. They rejoiced to be found worthy to suffer for the name of Christ and remained steadfast in their faith. On November 13, 1544, the judge sentenced them to death by burning at the stake.

Ursula refused to look away as Maria burned to death. She said, "Let me behold the end of my sister, for I also desire to receive the glory into which she shall enter." When given one last chance to recant, Ursula replied that her flesh was not too good to be burned for Christ.

Because she stood firm in her faith, Ursula died in the same manner as her sister-in-law, Maria.

Source: *The Bloody Theater or Martyrs Mirror of the Defenseless Christians*, twelfth edition, Thieleman J. van Braght, translated by Joseph F. Sohm in 1886, Herald Press, 1979.

Hans Denck (1495-1527)

Hans (Johann) Denck was born at Habach, near Huglfing in Upper Bavaria, Germany, in 1495. He was taught the faith by his parents and in 1519 received a Bachelor of Arts degree from the University of Ingolstadt. Later he attended the University of Basel and became versed in Latin, Greek, and Hebrew. Considered a humanist scholar, Denck was greatly influenced by medieval mysticism and was burdened for the deepening of his own spirituality and that of the church.

Denck became an Anabaptist in 1525 and was banished from the city of Nürnberg and forever separated from his wife and children under the threat of imprisonment. He was expelled from several cities because of his Anabaptist beliefs, including Augsburg, Strasbourg, Bergazber, and Landau in the Palatinate. He resided in Worms for several months and helped publish a translation of the Old Testament prophets. In 1527 he visited Anabaptist congregations in South Germany and Switzerland and was one of three preachers commissioned "to comfort and teach" the believers in the Zurich and Basel areas of Switzerland. He died of the plague in Basel in September 1527.

Throughout his life, Denck stood apart from the main theological stream of Anabaptism. He lived his motto that "no one may truly know Christ except one who follows Him in life." His major contribution to the Anabaptist faith lay in the earnestness with which he contended for Christianity as discipleship, and in the beauty of his sincere Christian spirit. Denck was one of the few personalities of the sixteenth century who never indulged in controversy except with a heavy heart.

Denck authored eleven items during his short life, including his most important work, *Ordnung Gottes und der Creaturen Werk* (1526), in which he discussed such questions as predestination, hell, heaven, the Trinity, idolatry in the pomp of the churches, and the peace of God.

Sources: *The Mennonite Encyclopedia*, vol. 1-4, edited by Harold S. Bender, et al., Herald Press, 1955-1959; and *Anabaptism in Outline*, edited by Walter Klaassen, Herald Press, 1981.

Maeyken van Deventer

For practicing her Anabaptist faith, authorities apprehended Maeyken van Deventer in 1573 in Rotterdam, Holland. Her execution took place soon after her arrest. Maeyken van Deventer is remembered for the testament she left her four young children.

In a letter to her children, Albert, Johan, Egbert, and Truyken, she wrote, "My children in the flesh, I must leave you young; may the Most High permit us to meet in the world to come, which shall be done before long by the Father, who will paternally bless us with His most holy name.... Thank the Most High, that you had a mother who was found worthy to shed her blood for the name of the Lord, and who, through His great grace and mercy, may be counted as a witness or martyr."

Maeyken encouraged her children to "press through the strait gate, for strait and narrow is the way that leadeth unto life..." and also instructed them to "call the fear of the Lord your Father, and wisdom and understanding shall be your mother."

Little else is known about Maeyken van Deventer because a great fire gutted the Rotterdam city hall in 1600 and destroyed all records of martyr executions and death sentences kept there.

Source: *The Bloody Theater or Martyrs Mirror of the Defenseless Christians*, twelfth edition, Thieleman J. van Braght, translated by Joseph F. Sohm in 1886, Herald Press, 1979.

Conrad Grebel (1498-1526)

Conrad Grebel, cofounder of the Swiss Brethren, performed the first baptism of the Anabaptist movement. Born in 1498, the second of six children of Junker Jakob Grebel and his wife, Dorothea Fries, Conrad Grebel probably grew up in the castle at Gruningern, a few miles east of Zurich. His father was a highly successful businessman and magistrate during Grebel's boyhood days.

Grebel attended the University of Basel and studied in Paris under a royal scholarship from the king of France. For almost six years he was a student among the humanists of the universities but, because of personal quarrels, never secured any kind of a degree.

Grebel had personal quarrels with his own family as well. They bitterly opposed his Anabaptist theology and his marriage to a woman below his class. He also had disagreements with reform leader Zwingli, especially over the point of infant baptism. He refused to baptize his own two-week-old daughter in 1525 and, with a small, inspired group of friends, was the first to introduce believers' baptism as it is known today.

Though a few letters have been preserved, Grebel was not a well-documented leader. He published a poetic ode to the Reformation in 1522 but left few other writings. He died of the plague in July 1526 in Maienfeld in the canton of Grisons, where his oldest sister lived. Conrad Grebel sought reality in the spiritual life, a reality that was far removed from mere externalism or legalism. He sought to generate and maintain a deep inner spiritual life through a living faith and personal union in Christ. He earnestly sought to make this inner spiritual life effective in the daily experience of the Christian believer, in trust in God for daily needs, in love toward the believers, in separation from sin and the world, and in a life of holiness.

Sources: *The Mennonite Encyclopedia*, vol. 1–4, edited by Harold S. Bender, et al., Herald Press, 1955–1959; *The Mennonite Encyclopedia*, vol. 5, edited by Cornelius J. Dyck and Dennis D. Martin, Herald Press, 1990; and *Readings from Mennonite Writings New and Old*, J. Craig Haas, Good Books, 1992.

Balthasar Hubmaier (1480-1528)

Balthasar Hubmaier was one of the first Anabaptist leaders to have his writings appear in a full scholarly modern German edition. He was the only Anabaptist leader with a public career of any significance in his earlier Catholic experience.

Born sometime after 1480 in Friedenberg near Augsburg, Germany, Hubmaier was educated at the universities of Friedberg and Ingolstadt. At Ingolstadt he was both the prorector and lecturer in theology before becoming cathedral preacher at Regensburg. In 1521, Hubmaier became pastor at Waldshut. While there he began to embrace certain Reformation concepts and by Easter 1525 he was baptized along with sixty of his parishioners. He, in turn, baptized three hundred other Anabaptists.

Though he was a participant in the Anabaptist wing of the Reformation for less than three years, Hubmaier's writings and public activity gained him a well-earned reputation as the most learned and the most gifted communicator among the Anabaptists. His theological training prepared him for point-by-point debates on issues such as free will, original sin, and infant baptism. His motto was "The truth is immortal," and his striving for it was evident in his numerous writings and teachings, the course of his life, and ultimately, his death at the stake in Vienna on March 10, 1528.

Hubmaier can be considered the theologian of the "new birth," for he was the first to articulate clearly the concept that has become basic in Anabaptist and Mennonite self-understanding. His published works in German and English still stimulate and challenge those who, like Hubmaier, hold to believers' baptism.

Sources: *The Mennonite Encyclopedia*, vol. 5, edited by Cornelius J. Dyck and Dennis D. Martin, Herald Press, 1990; *Balthasar Hubmaier: Theologian of Anabaptism*, translated and edited by H. Wayne Pipkin and John H. Yoder, Herald Press, 1989; and *Anabaptism in Outline*, edited by Walter Klaassen, Herald Press, 1981.

Hutterian Brethren

Hutterian Brethren practice community of goods following the example of the first Christian community: "All that believed were together, and had all things in common" (Acts 2:44). First established in Moravia in 1529, the Hutterian Brethren were re-established in 1533 by Jakob Hutter.

Today Hutterian colonies exist mainly in the following places: British Columbia, Alberta, Saskatchewan, Manitoba, Washington, Montana, North Dakota, South Dakota, Minnesota, Pennsylvania, New York, Connecticut, England, and Japan.

The Hutterian Brethren movement experienced renewed unity in 1974, and since then Hutterian Brethren have felt urged to share this unity with others. With this intention, brothers and sisters from eastern and western Bruderhofs (communities) have participated jointly in meetings and conferences with Mennonites and other Christian and Jewish community movements. Their purpose is to learn from other groups' histories what the radical message of Jesus means in the late twentieth century.

Sources: *The Mennonite Encyclopedia*, vol. 5, edited by Cornelius J. Dyck and Dennis D. Martin, Herald Press, 1990.

Felix Manz (1498-1527)

Born in 1498 in Zurich, Switzerland, the son of a canon of the cathedral church, Felix Manz is best known as a cofounder of the Swiss Brethren and the first Anabaptist martyr.

He was an avid follower of Reformation leader Zwingli from 1519 until 1523, when differences in opinion on infant baptism and tithes became irreconcilable. Manz joined Conrad Grebel, and they began a zealous movement promoting believers' baptism.

Felix Manz was well educated and a good Hebrew scholar. He was repeatedly arrested for proclaiming the new doctrine, and even held Bible readings in his mother's house after being banned from the state church.

Because he refused to cease preaching and baptizing, Manz became the first Anabaptist martyr on January 5,

1527. He was taken from the Wellenberg prison to Lake Zurich down the Limmat, placed in a boat and rowed out in the water. Hearing encouragement from his mother and brother along the shore, Manz prayed his last prayer, "Father, into Thy hands I commend my soul," and with his hands tied to his knees, he was tossed overboard.

While he left no published writings, recent research indicates that the *Protestation und Schutzschrift*, earlier attributed to Conrad Grebel, may have been written by Felix Manz. He wrote the song "I sing with exultation," after participating in the first Anabaptist baptism in January 1525.

Sources: *The Mennonite Encyclopedia*, vol. 1–4, edited by Harold S. Bender, et al., Herald Press, 1955–1959; *Smith's Story of the Mennonites*, C. Henry Smith, Faith & Life Press, 1981; and *Readings from Mennonite Writings New and Old*, J. Craig Haas, Good Books, 1992.

Pilgram Marpeck (?-1556)

Pilgram Marpeck was an author and leader of the South German Anabaptists from 1530 to 1556. A native of Tyrol, Austria, it is possible that Marpeck grew up in the Bavarian town of Rosenheim and moved to Rattenberg, Austria, where his father Heinrich served as a councilman, mayor, and district magistrate. He attended Latin school in Rattenberg and received a "scholarly education" which can be discerned from his writings.

Professionally, Marpeck worked in the city hospital, organized the city's crossbow competition, and acted as purchasing agent for the mining guild's infirmary before entering office as mining magistrate in 1525. He became an Anabaptist, and in 1528 he was removed from office for refusing to aid in catching Anabaptists as requested by Innsbruck authorities.

From 1532-1544, Marpeck resided in Switzerland and traveled to Tyrol, Moravia, South Germany, and Alsace where he established congregations and had contact with the Hutterites and Swiss Brethren. By 1544 he was working in Augsburg's city forest and later as city engineer there. Although warned three times to desist from Anabaptist activity, he participated in the leadership of a group which met in his home, which was on public property. He continued significant correspondence with Anabaptist groups in Switzerland, Alsace, South Germany, and Moravia.

Pilgram Marpeck had one daughter, Margareth, with his first wife, Sophia. When Sophia died, Marpeck married Anna and they adopted three children. He died a natural death in Augsburg in 1556.

Four anonymous works have been attributed to Marpeck. They include *Clear Response*, *Clear and Useful Instruction*, *The Exposure of the Babylonian Whore*, and *Confession*. Marpeck affirmed the divinity of Christ, but stressed Christ's historical, physical humanity. Marpeck believed that the Bible is properly understood only in the context of and by the whole community of believers.

Sources: *The Mennonite Encyclopedia*, vol. 5, edited by Cornelius J. Dyck and Dennis D. Martin, Herald Press, 1990; and *Anabaptism in Outline*, edited by Walter Klaassen, Herald Press, 1981.

Michael Sattler (1490-1527)

Michael Sattler was born sometime around 1490 at Stauffen in Breisgau, Germany. He entered the Benedictine Monastery of St. Peter's but in the 1520s came, by way of Lutheran and Zwinglian ideas, to forsake the monastery and marry Margaretha, a former Benguine sister.

The life and work of Michael Sattler has been recognized as pivotal to the self-definition and subsequent survival of Swiss Anabaptism. He is credited with primary responsibility as author of the Schleitheim Confession which addresses the perplexing issues the Mennonites dealt with and were united through, during that time. The seven articles of the Schleitheim Confession outlined decisions made concerning the following topics: baptism, ban, the breaking of bread, separation from abomination, shepherds or leaders in the congregation, the sword, and the oath. The articles circulated widely together with vivid accounts of Sattler's heroic martyrdom which occurred on May 20, 1527, at Rottenburg am Neckar, Germany.

Sattler had traveled to Wurttemberg, apparently to pastor the congregation at Horb, immediately after the Schleitheim meetings which had taken place February 24, 1527. He was arrested in Horb for his Anabaptist beliefs, along with several other Anabaptists, including his wife. His sentence was to be led through the market, have his tongue cut off, his body gripped six times with red-hot tongs, and then be thrown alive into a fire with a keg of gunpowder around his neck. Sentenced on Saturday, Sattler was not executed until Monday.

Sattler praised God at the place of his execution, as he was being tied to the ladder with cords. A small sack of gunpowder, hung around his neck, exploded when he was thrown into the fire. As he burned, he became unbound in the fire and raised his arms high with the first two fingers on each hand outstretched and cried with a powerful voice: "Father, into thy hands I commend my soul!" That night, many observed the sun and the moon standing still with golden letters written within. Such a bright light went out from them that many thought it was midday.

Sources: ***The Legacy of Michael Sattler***, John H. Yoder, Herald Press, 1973; ***Readings from Mennonite Writings New and Old***, J. Craig Haas, Good Books, 1992; and ***The Mennonite Encyclopedia***, vol. 5, edited by Cornelius J. Dyck and Dennis D. Martin, Herald Press, 1990.

Menno Simons (1496-1561)

Menno Simons, of peasant origin, was born in 1496 in the Frisian village of Witmarsum, Holland, a few miles inland from the North Sea coast. From this humble beginning came the man who became the most influential Anabaptist leader.

His followers are called Mennonites.

Scholars have long agreed that Menno Simons was not the founder but the organizer of Dutch Mennonitism. It is generally agreed that Menno initially was a Melchiorite, a follower of Melchior Hoffman, and that he called the Munster Anabaptists "brothers" but broke decisively with them over the use of force to bring in the kingdom of God.

No single organizing center of Menno's thought has been identified but there is general agreement that he moved from a stress upon conversion early in his career to a gradually increasing emphasis on the church which, in turn, led to greater emphasis on discipline. The vision of a pure church also led Menno to stress the heavenly origin of the human Christ, a doctrine which caused much controversy already in his time, but has more recently been affirmed as a vital part of Menno's understanding of salvation and the possibility of believers becoming Christ-like.

Menno Simons died of natural causes in January 1561 at the age of sixty-five. He had chosen as his final resting place the little Anabaptist village of Weustenfeld in Holstein, Germany. According to a custom not unknown to the Anabaptists of that day, he was buried in his own garden. The location, remembered by an old Mennonite family of Hamburg, was marked with an appropriate monument by the church at Hamburg in 1902.

Though he never saw himself in the role, Menno Simons was a molder of tradition. He was concerned above all to be faithful to "the heavenly vision" and his own circle saw him as a faithful witness. There are hints that he regretted decisions he made, which, nevertheless, lived on in their consequences. Still, what he wrote and did lived beyond him and became part of an ongoing tradition.

Sources: *Readings from Mennonite Writings New and Old*, J. Craig Haas, Good Books, 1992; *The Mennonite Encyclopedia*, vol. 1–4, edited by Harold S. Bender, et al., Herald Press, 1955–1959; and *Smith's Story of the Mennonites*, C. Henry Smith, Faith & Life Press, 1981.